A Journal of Love

Meditations on John's Gospel and Letters

A Journal of

Meditations on John's Gospel and Letters

PAMELA SMITH, SS.C.M.

Dedication

For the adorers
in Danville and Charleston

The Scripture passages contained herein are from the *New Revised Standard Version of the Bible*, ©1989, by the Division of Christian Education of the National Council of Churches of Christ in the U.S.A. Used by permission. All rights reserved.

Twenty-Third Publications
A Division of Bayard
One Montauk Avenue, Suite 200
New London, CT 06320
(860) 437-3013 or (800) 321-0411
www.twentythirdpublications.com

Copyright ©2006 Pamela Smith, SS.C.M. All rights reserved. No part of this publication may be reproduced in any manner without prior written permission of the publisher. Write to the Permissions Editor.

ISBN-10: 1-58595-537-X
ISBN 978-158595-557-4
Library of Congress Catalog Card Number: 2005929694
Printed in the U.S.A.

Contents

Introduction

Sometimes, in a rare moment, a person falls in love with an idea and pursues it unto death. It may be a theory of how trees or their apples fall, how traits are passed from generation to generation, or how the world changes in climactic leaps. It may be a notion of how melodic lines interweave in grand and unexpected orchestral settings. It may be a whim about the play of color and light and sweep of brush. It may be curiosity about the work of words upon human themes. Such fallings in love have brought us Newton, Einstein, Mendel, Barbara McClintock, and Rachel Carson; Mozart, the Schumanns, Stravinsky, and John Cage; Michelangelo, Van Gogh, Mary Cassatt, Picasso, and Georgia O'Keefe; Shakespeare and Toni Morrison, Chaucer and Alice Walker, William Langland and Mary Oliver. The world is full of geniuses who have fallen in love with their gift and theme.

Beyond these fallings in love, though, lies the force (energy) that changes history, brings beings to life, wages war, builds religions, moves frontiers, upheaves plans, propels the sane and stable into frenzy, sends shock waves across centuries. What drives desire and dreams is the trauma and thrill and magnificence of falling in love with an extraordinary and unexpected person. When that person seems also to be more than a human being, the pulse beat of love cannot abate with time.

That is what happened for John the evangelist, John the Divine. What transpired for him and in him was what Bernard Lonergan has called that "otherworldly falling in love," which is the deepest form of religious conversion.

The movement from idea and ideal to person to love-driven life-change was the journey of the legendary apostle John. He had the energy and idealism to fall in love with a messianic idea early on. What gripped him, though, and fired his life was falling in love with the charismatic rabbi who became, for him, simultaneously friend and Word. What imprinted him upon the ages, as well as upon chapter and verse of holy texts, was that the beloved friend was found to be Messiah, Redeemer, and God-come-down. John, who knew he was beloved of this Beloved, was caught up in a dramatic and never-to-be-repeated revelation.

Entering into the Gospel of John and the three epistles simply, starkly, step by step, is to embark on an adventure, a long and thrilling walk into the story of a great and unsurpassable love, the Love that John discovered was God's name. Following word by word, without the accretions and distractions of exegesis and critical scrutiny, is not to demean deep study and not to deny linguistic, historical, or theological insights. It is, instead, a request for one pure thing: an encounter, a felt sense of what it must have been to live that love.

John's Gospel and Letters as Journal of Love

Pious tradition tells us that the Gospel according to John comes down, in the Greek, from oral history, oft-repeated story, high-flying theologizing about the Jesus event in texts collected and redacted between 90 and 100 C.E. Scholarly review suggests a Gentile audience, an identification with the community of one known as the "beloved disciple," and a reverence for the name and tradition of John. Tradition has him the youngest of the apostles; he was a son of Zebedee, a fisherman who was eyewitness to the most critical turning points in the mission of the Galilean called the Christ. Tradition also says that he was the longest lived, charged with the care of the rabbi's mother, associated with the early Christians in Ephesus, revered as an expert and elder, and then exiled as an old man on Patmos. John was visionary, obsessed with the themes of love and community, stridently opposed to the body-soul dualism of the Gnostics, even while launching into ecstatic praise of the life beyond this one. At one time in his life, he was star-struck and intimate enough to draw close to Jesus, to rest there and get his ear. John was contemplative, mystic, and lover. From being disciple and best friend, he was becoming apostle and saint.

Mystics lovers, and saints, we know, do all sorts of uncommon things to express their love. They sing to one another and write sonnets. They write alphabetical descriptions of why they love—proclaiming that the other person is affectionate, beautiful, compassionate, everything that one ever hoped for, scintillating, true, understanding, and vibrant. John, or whoever scribed in his name, pronounced his love philosophically. The One who came, the one and only, was the first and last word, the alpha and omega. He was "I Am," life itself, and could only be symbolized by ordinary things when they were understood in extraordinary ways: water, bridegroom, gate, sheepfold, shepherd, bread, resurrection, way.

What this love did to John was what only a great love can do: offer him abundant life; set his direction and pace in deep meaning; fire him with undying passion. No action he could take, no story he could tell, no memory he could share, no cup he could ever sip and pass, no words he could ever shape would be enough. John began with the beginning, and when he stopped could only say, "But there are also many other things that Jesus did; if every one of them were written down, I suppose that the world itself could not contain the books that would be written" (Jn 21:25).

The only way to begin to grasp what the turns and twists and simplicities and mysteries of his text mean is to be in love and to read in love. That is what I propose to do. And that is what I invite the reader to do: To follow along with the unshaded eyes of a lover, imagining all the while what it must be like to be full of a dream. To remember everything that one has ever known of love and then expand it more and more, discovering that one's love radiates into the encompassing circle of divinity. To dwell on what it might mean to be in love with a magnetic personality, a great teacher, and wondrous friend, and to wonder, hope, and finally know that this vibrant human is also the fullness of God.

An Overview of the Fourth Gospel

When you read the whole gospel rapidly, he explodes upon the scene, this Jesus, clear and arcane, charming and dismaying, heaven-sent and mission-bent. He reads minds, he knows hearts, he changes everything, he understands far beyond the mundane. He bothers much about some small things and little about some things that would seem large and eventful. A wake of confusion flows out behind him. Yet a Samaritan woman, a paralytic, a blind man, a woman caught in adultery, a fusspot named Martha, and a stinking dead man all receive life, hope, assurance, and clear direction from him. He is altogether too much, and thus John raves about light.

There's an edge and an urgency to what Jesus does and says. The edge is this suggestion: You can, too. You can be light, do God's deeds (Jn 3:21), look around and see when the harvest is ripe for gathering (4:35). You can believe (6:29), eat the bread (6:51), drink the living water (7:37). You can stay in the word, know the truth, and be free (8:31–32). You can follow and serve (12:26), wash each other's feet (13:14), love one another (13:34), and ask things of God, using Love's name (14:13). You can be free of trouble and fear (15:27), and you have the strength to let no one steal your joy (16:22). You can have peace and take courage (16:33). You can receive the Spirit (20:22) and, in fact, be the Spirit vibrant in the world (14:17). Just love (15:12).

Such are the timeless messages the beloved disciple heard in the teacher's clear and certain voice. He heard urgency, too, an urgency that declared the time ever now (5:25) and "always here" (7:6). So go ahead, the voice said. Do.

God of vision and of sweeping change, have your way with me so I may be and fulfill all that you see in me. Let me know the gospel truth about my power, when I am infused with you.

For Reflection

I am so often on standby, so often on hold. How do I know when the time has come to act, to use my gifts, to release the power of baptism and of the Spirit within me? Can I recall a time when I assuredly knew that I had power beyond my own and was able to claim it and use it?

Celestial Hymn

John 1:1–18

All things came into being through him,
and without him not one thing came into being.

"You Are My Everything," declares a golden oldie. Robert Goulet, in Camelot's "If Ever I Would Leave You," sings out that there is no season when it is possible to leave a great love. And Tina Turner sings, "You're simply the best/Better than all the rest" to an imagined great flame. An unparalleled love pledges itself, is exuberant, exaggerates, and sets the beloved at the center of the universe. There is no way and no time we can conceive of not being in love. No one is better, and no one can ever take our one and only's place. The harmony of the spheres, the music of the universe is played, as far as we are concerned, in our loved one's key.

Stretch that, then, to the cosmic and divine. If we have fallen in love as the beloved disciple did, we know that nothing can exist without that love. If love is the Word, the Word comes first, imagining all, making all, being in all. The Word comes last, as well. Before, during, and after somehow blur because in love time stops. All is love, and all is now, explosion upon explosion of it.

That is why John's gospel begins with the near-nonsense vocabulary of mysticism. In the beginning, love was. Love was with. Love was God. It was dark. Love went unnoticed. But love shone. The light of love then suddenly broke upon everything. People could see, and indeed did, when their eyes opened. They received when they saw, when they let themselves be flooded with seeing. They needed only to hold on to the refulgence. Filled to overflowing, they broke into a hymn.

Out of time and yet today, the gospel tells, the same holds true. Love breaks upon us and makes us. Love sets us aglow—yet only, curiously enough, if we wish that love do so. That is the way with courting and romance and consummation. There is invitation, attraction, and, in the end, will. That is the way, too, with a revelation of God.

If we will ourselves to love, we discover that later, when we wish to tell about it, we lack language. We speak in analogies, abstractions: word, light, power, truth, grace upon grace, nearness to God's heart.

Whatever we say, it can never be enough. All that love does, after all, is too much. So we write a Logos hymn, as the beginning of this gospel (1:1–5) has been called. Likely we have hummed it to ourselves before we had the words.

God, catch me up in the swirl of your coming, in the timelessness and constancy of the One who has your heart and now has mine. Instill in me the certainty that before I had met love, my beloved life had already begun. As I encounter love now and forever in the person of your Son, let me begin anew, again and again. May I always sing your song.

For Reflection

The experienced reader of Scripture notices right away that there are no infancy stories of Jesus here. What am I to make of that lack? Does it create a void? Does the "Logos hymn" somehow fill it in? What light does this beginning shed on the coming of Christ that the stories of Bethlehem might not? What does this hymn sing to me?

To Announce, Then Disappear

John 1:6–9, 15, 19–28

"I am the voice of one crying out in the wilderness."

Beth Moore, in *The Beloved Disciple,* makes a sharp observation about that earlier John, the baptizer, the cousin, the precursor. That John knew who he was himself and who he wasn't. He was the one who had a ministry and a mission that was somehow all preliminary, a task of preparation and a prophetic voice given so that he could call others to attention and call them to reform. He wasn't the Messiah. He wasn't the one to whom they were to attach lasting allegiance, though he had his disciples. He was called to attract, to teach, to lead, and then to set free, as he gave way to the Christ.

When asked the question who or what we are, most of us launch into job descriptions. I'm teacher, writer, administrator, let's say. Or we identify ourselves by state in life and place in church and family. I'm a religious sister and a blood sister, firstborn, baptized with a first name spun oddly off of one saint and a second name borrowed directly from another. If we have any depth, or if we have been gripped in a compelling relationship, we may pause and add what is so personal that we add it hesitantly: Oh, yes: I'm also friend and lover. We'll mention it, that is, if love is at present preoccupying us, and if we're fearless and free enough. What takes us longer, sad to say, is to enunciate what ought to be, and what really is, our core identity: I'm creature of the universe, member of planet Earth, child of God, follower and friend of Jesus, a spiritual seeker who is Spirit-led.

We know readily, it seems, what we are not: genius, saint, super-Mom, gold medallist, queen of the world. Not whole, not entirely intact, not even consistent: that's how most of us might self-describe, if we're honest. Even so, we are loathe to say what we're fundamentally lacking, what we really are not: believers who are wholly given over to God.

John the Baptizer stands out because he was precisely that: given over, swallowed up, all for God. If we have ever been swallowed up in love, if we have ever let everything we are and own go for love, we have a hint of how it might be. All of our self-definitions dwarf, and all of our pretenses fail. The Baptizer let himself be voice and sign and song with no illusions, no assertions of self-importance. Before he began his holy task, he had already been transformed.

The question for us is when will we finally loosen our grips and surrender our goals sufficiently that others might see past us—and sufficiently that we might serve dispensably? Only a great love can pry away what we still hold tightly. Only a great love can coax us to give over what we clutch closer than close. John's life is testimony that we can be so intimately devoted and so ready to bend and make way if we grasp that we are deeply needed and deeply loved—and that we have been so, long before we arrived at the great day.

Let me hear it, Lord: "Among you stands one whom you do not know" (1:26). I think I do. I thought I did. Now let me know what I am to do and where I must let go. Let me know who stood as first love, long before my noticing.

For Reflection

John the Baptizer holds ambiguous importance. On the one hand, he is the last of the Hebrew prophets and greatest among them. On the other hand, he is the star of the warm-up act in a great theater, given a moment's spotlight, billed small, and primed to disappear. In what way am I called to a great mission and the delivery of a compelling message and yet primed to disappear?

Dove, Fig Tree, and the Art of Seeing

John 1:29–51

The next day...The next day...The next day...

Cingular cellphones, when they first light up, bear the image of two pure white doves aloft, their wings seeming to touch, in a light whisper of apparent motion. The effect is one of light, speed, closeness, and delicacy.

The one dove mentioned in the gospel record of proclamation and call set off not just an airy ripple but a sonic boom of effects. The Baptizer testified that Jesus was the Son of God, the one on whom the Holy Spirit had descended and remained, the one whom his disciples—including Andrew and, quite likely, the young John—had unknowingly awaited. Events moved with the haste and acceleration of love at first sight. One day these disciples were invited by rabbi Jesus to "come and see," to meet him on home turf, in a more intimate setting. They remembered the details and the time—around four in the afternoon.

A day later, this rabbi and Lamb found Philip. Meanwhile, Andrew had gathered up Peter. Philip rousted out Nathanael. Jesus enigmatically remarked to the latter that he had already seen him under a fig tree. No one guessed at the meaning, but Nathanael's reaction suggested that somehow Jesus had read his mind, his heart, and the longing which underlay all his deeds.

Jesus saw something far subtler than the person visible beneath that fig tree.

This part of the gospel of John is, of course, more about seeing than reading. The Baptizer saw the Spirit descend like a dove. Andrew and his companion came and saw the Spirit-filled master. Peter received Andrew's eyewitness testimony and came to see for himself. Jesus saw Philip and beckoned, and Philip responded when his eye caught the beckoning. Philip, in turn, caught sight of Nathanael, only to learn that Jesus had already been on the lookout, too, for him.

There was something compelling, the evangelist reveals, in the look, the welcoming glance, the steady gaze, and the eagle-eye insight of this one they called Rabbi, Lamb, Son of God, Son of Man. He had, par excellence, the look of love.

And love's look, we know, when it is deep, searching, and genuine, sees into, sees through, reads the text of the beloved's yearning, looks with delight, and foresees possibility. "You will see heaven opened and the angels of God ascending and descending," Jesus promised to those who first saw him and followed (1:51). They were caught in the cross-hairs of his sight, stunned and dovestruck.

Spirit of God, catch my attention so I may look on the One who sees through me. Focus the lens of my longing and looking with your precision.

For Reflection

When have I found myself in a situation, or called to some project or mission, and had a sense that I was somehow destined to this from the beginning? How has God figured in my understanding of what I was about? How did I understand my freedom within God's plan?

Have I ever known someone who seemed to be able to read me through and through? What has such an experience meant to me and taught me? Do I understand God as knowing me even more deeply?

The Cana Hour

John 2:1–11

When the wine gave out, the mother of Jesus said to him, "They have no wine."

We all have built into us a sense of timing about certain matters, a sense of rightness and ripeness of the moment, an instinct about when to set forth and when to hold back. That intuitive sense of athletic gunshot—Now!—jump-starts us, especially if we are strong, determined personalities programmed for the sprint. Similarly, the competitors' caution—Not yet!—must be heeded and can only rarely be overridden because we know there are penalties for a false start. Only the intervention of a higher authority, the maneuverings of irreversible circumstance, or the bonds of compelling human affection can get us to launch into something when we think it premature.

At Cana, Jesus found himself in a quandary. His inner clock ticked to an "hour" he was quite sure had not yet come. But a couple, clearly people he knew and perhaps had grown up with, faced embarrassment. It was, perhaps, a small thing. But it could have been seen as a breach of hospitality, a careless negligence, to run out of wine at a wedding feast. So, there was his mother's plea. And then her adamant certainty that he would do something to save the day—or at least, for the sake of bride and groom, save face. "Do whatever he tells you," she said, ignoring his rebuff and confident that his resolve would give way (2:5).

Perhaps it was not just a case of a strong man's being overruled by a stronger mother. Perhaps, instead, her intervention persuaded him that something beyond the celebration was going on. Perhaps she was edging him toward an outbreak of power which he knew was surely to come but for which he felt unready. Perhaps his clock had been losing time amid the hurly-burly, and hers was set to some sort of heavenly Greenwich. Perhaps she understood, by her mix of Spirit-impulse, angel-voice, and woman's intuition, that some hour had, after all, come.

His mother was not one for exalted claims or power plays. She was usually more a background person, one who fancied herself part of the large supporting cast of faithful Jews who would, by quiet strength, help usher in the Kingdom.

There was something timely, and something about her son's timing, connected with this wedding feast, she sensed. Something was awaiting them—an act of God, the demand of the occasion, a grand gesture of love. Whatever it was, the large vats of water were drawn. Whatever it was, he spoke them into splendid wine.

And so a dumbfounded disciple named it "the first of his signs" (2:11).

God, attune me always to your timing. Hour by hour take whatever is water in me and make it into holy wine.

For Reflection

When have I undergone a change of mind about the timing of something important—a job change, the fulfillment of a request, a trip, a major shift in the way I spend my energy? What has occasioned the change of direction and change of heart in me?

Temple Home

John 2:12–25

His disciples remembered that it was written,
"Zeal for your house will consume me."

In between bursts of activity, Jesus spent a few days at home. With the wedding over, the wine drunk, a long mission journey ahead, and the Passover yet to be, he seemed ready for a slowing, for a spell of rest. Thus what came next could not have been expected: a routing of money-changers, a roughneck driving of cattle and sheep, an uproar in the temple precincts. All of this followed in the aftermath of a few days of eating home-baked bread, dipping it leisurely in his mother's stores of olive oil, and telling some old family stories to his still rather green disciples.

The whole idea of home exploded for them. A line of psalm came back, hauntingly, about zeal for the temple, zeal for the place where God dwells. They thought of it as they gossiped among themselves about his shouting at the dove-sellers. "Maybe this is what it meant," they speculated. "Maybe we're supposed to think of God's house as home. Maybe we're supposed to realize that some things trivialize and even defile it." It was as certain as their heritage that God was understood to dwell in David's dream, Solomon's capstone, Judaism's ideal, the temple. "Where God is at home," they mumbled, "it likely isn't fitting to crowd marketplace, currency exchange, and barnyard." That must have been what Jesus' knockabout behavior was about.

They had heard him speak of another temple, too—one's own holy body. There, too, he taught, God dwelled. A person's body, he showed them by example, needs silent spaces, sanctuaries, elegant corners where law and prophets are sung without the background din of the everyday.

Easy, reverent, at-homeness, and a consecrated site where one could hear God's quietude—that was what Jesus longed for. That was what he sought for his followers. That was what he found where his mother was. Of all places, he thought, one ought to find a hushed waiting for God on God's holy mountain, in God's temple. When he did not find it there, it angered him.

The disciples mulled this over and remembered. Love also has its wrath, they learned.

Let me save my anger, God, to energize a rightful fight for love. Let any anger I feel always urge me home.

For Reflection

The Holy Spirit is the giver of zeal. When have I found within me the zeal to carry out a challenging task? Has it been more a matter of performing an act of love that stretched me to my limits, taking on an issue that was controversial and might carry risk for me, or simply working very hard over the long haul? What were the sources of strength that comforted and encouraged me? How did I envision God amid the difficulty?

Inching Toward Birth

John 3:1–21

"The wind blows where it chooses, and you hear the sound of it,
but you do not know where it comes from or where it goes.
So it is with everyone who is born of the Spirit."

There are admirers, followers, potential lovers who watch from the sidelines, measure their words, and make furtive inquiries about the other (his or her ideas, accomplishments, responses to situations, whereabouts). They control their faces, feign disinterest, mask their eagerness as newsy curiosity, and wait before they make a move. They are like the child who tiptoes into the ocean, testing the pull and temperature, uneasy about being caught in the cold or undertow.

Nicodemus was one of those. When he finally sought Jesus out by night, Nicodemus, seeker of truth, already knew that he was attracted to and practically convinced by this rabbi. Yet he wanted an excuse to remain noncommittal. The "born again" message he received from Jesus may have baffled him. It may have given him just the excuse he needed, too, to hang back.

What Jesus meant, it seems, is this: "Nicodemus, give it all up. Start again. Forget your prized role as Pharisee and quit fretting about what the others will think. Stop skulking about in the dark. Follow your heart, and you'll follow me."

One thing about those lovers and seekers who try and test and collect data and stalk: they do persist.

Nicodemus' face to face with Jesus was an almost-but-not-quite event. Like the rich young man, he could have backed away, unwilling to abandon the security of the familiar. Then again, like Levi the tax collector, he could have thrown it all over at a word and simply come. We know that he did not wholeheartedly commit but chose a cautious middle course. When Nicodemus next appears in the gospel, he is suggesting that Jesus, who had caused displeasure by a Sabbath healing and raising messianic hopes, deserved a hearing such as the law had determined. After this episode, which ends with Nicodemus being mocked as a Galilean sympathizer, he does not reappear until it is time to claim a body, after the crucifixion.

What went on in the interim of these appearances, we can only guess. It seems, though, that Nicodemus straddled two worlds. What the two worlds held in common was the conviction that they were propagating and preserving what God intended for his chosen. Both believed they were searching law and prophets and living their hearts. Both had a passion for God and God's promises.

In the end, Nicodemus chose the newer and more open world, that of Jesus and his disciples. He came bearing a hundred pounds of aloes and myrrh to help carry Jesus' body to the Arimathean's waiting tomb. He remembered the rebirth Jesus had spoken of. All he could do in the end was hope that he had not come so late that he'd be stillborn.

Lord, help me heed your invitations and your tough urgings in good time so that I may come to new birth and full life. Ease the contractions that free me to life, and make real in me the power of baptism.

For Reflection

Nicodemus clearly lived a dark night. In the end, we hope that he was towed into new day with the events of Easter and Pentecost. Yet we cannot say. When have I experienced or witnessed a dark night of mind and soul? What occasioned it—doubt, disappointment, dread, something else? How was I delivered from it?

Countryside Time

John 3:22–36

After this Jesus and his disciples went into the Judean countryside, and he spent some time there with them and baptized.

Cousin John, meanwhile, continued baptizing—at Aenon, near Salim, it says, because there was a great water supply there. The dispute about who ought to be baptizing arose, and the dispute, too, about who ought to be collecting disciples. The Baptizer deferred, of course, to Jesus: "He must increase" (3:30). He referred to Jesus as "from above," "from heaven," from the Father, imparting the Spirit. All of this, including John's deferential response, the disciples of Jesus remembered. It was a testimony to John's lasting import as well as his right to call, to initiate, to gather followers, to speak God's word, and to prepare the way.

Jesus' disciples, in the meantime, were still obviously trying to figure him out. The Baptizer had embraced Jesus in faith even while holding to his semi-independent mission. The disciples of Jesus had begun baptizing, too, even if they were not entirely sure what they were baptizing the masses or the ragtag into—or why.

What was most important in this ongoing chronicle of call, response, confusion, clarification, faltering, and adverting to the Father was what preceded it: the time Jesus spent with them. Nothing has been recorded of what the disciples and Jesus said and did in an out of the way region of Judea. It may actually have been little more than simply being together without an agenda. Nothing is recorded of travelogue, discourse, no "I am" declarations, no mystifying challenge or warning. There is just this remark about the Judean countryside and some undefined time spent.

Anyone who has gone apart to a woodland retreat, a beach house, a campground, a fishing lodge, a bed and breakfast on a side road, or a quiet cabin with a loved one knows, however, what that means. There's time to notice how mist rises in the morning and where light first strikes a hillside. There's time to watch how thinly or fully streams flow, to locate the whereabouts of wells and springs, or to gauge the timing of the tides. There's opportunity to note the crease marks on a beloved's face and to observe how they change with concentration, laughter, a moment's pain, or a stir of memory.

Whatever else ensued, we know that what followed with the Baptizer seemed monumentally important in the aftermath of intimate time together. Their attentiveness to what came next had been primed by what went before.

They were in the midst of mystery, for sure. But they also remembered that the Master, still so unknown, still so undecipherable in so many ways, had taken time to eat with them, wash in local water, chat lightly when the stars came out, and snore within their hearing. For a short time, they had had no public displays, no earth-shaking messages, no clamor of crowds. They had simply had the look on his face, the steadiness of his gait, the assurance that when he moved on, he would take them with him. They were ready to understand better the deference and the determination of his cousin.

Lord, let me learn more of you and be ready for more of you still as you offer me down time, friend time, and countryside days. Attune me to your person, your being, your laughter and sighs, as well as to your words and works.

For Reflection

In what areas of my life must I decrease to assure that evidence of the Lord's power and presence increases? How and where do I find friendship time with the Lord?

Encounter at the Well

John 4:1–42

The woman said to him, "I know that Messiah is coming."

Jesus wanted whole hearts, undivided attention, but he was not a jealous or possessive lover. He could strike up a conversation against all propriety with a solitary woman at a well. He could know very well of her five husbands and current live-in and still speak about worship, spirit, and truth. He could disclose himself to her and invite her to living water whether or not she registered any willingness to change or adapt. He took her on her own terms. He encountered and even embraced her loneliness, her bravado, her brokenness, her masks, and her underlying insecurity. He raised the bar in his level of dialogue with her, refusing to talk about where she might better measure up but instead addressing her on an intellectual and spiritual plane.

In the other gospels, Jesus took pains to guard what scholars have called the "messianic secret." He dodged the clear unveiling of his identity. Here, though, with this woman who seemingly lacked stability, credibility, and morality, he unabashedly identified himself. When she spoke of the Messiah to come, he matter-of-factly declared, "I am he" (4:26).

We may presume that this encounter with Jesus changed everything for this woman of Samaria. Yet he required nothing of her, and all that is recorded is that she announced the good news of his arrival to the nearby townspeople. We know only that she left her water jar behind at the well. It may merely have been a sign of her astonishment. It may simply have been a practical measure to gain a footloose quickness to her step as she hastened to tell someone, anyone, that the Messiah appeared to be in their midst. Then again, the abandoned water jar may have been symbolic of her transformation, her freedom, finally, to leave behind what she had thought of as a life source and personal necessity.

We may never know the whole of her story. What we do know is that Jesus gave everything and asked very little. A swig of freshly drawn water. A few moments of conversation. A draught of loving attention. This small movement on his part seems to us, hearing the story so much later, to have been enough to shift the tectonic plates of one woman's earthy soul.

Casual drifter, waiting by my local well, see through me and take the little of myself that I can offer. Let me in on the secret that you know me, love me in my ceaseless searchings and wrong turns, and can, by slightest urging, raise me to my better, truer self. Free me of my false dependencies.

For Reflection

What is it really that has gone terribly wrong in my life? Can I entrust it to God? Do I trust a gentle response? In spite of my dependencies, my deflected ideals, my wayward surrenders, can I converse with God about my deepest desires and most noble dreams? If the Lord seems at times a stranger to me, can I open myself anyway and trust his compassion?

A Sign of Healing

John 4:43–54

And they said to him, "Yesterday at one in the afternoon the fever left him."

Ready or not, certain or not, we will try almost anything for the sake of life and health, especially for a child. We will consent to new chemotherapies, conduct Miracle Network fundraisers, get second, third, and fourth opinions, rearrange our work lives, take out loans, travel to clinics across the country, enlist prayer partners, seek out faith healers, and make pilgrimages to grottos where restoring waters bubble up.

Jesus was the royal official's last chance. He had heard about the water and wine, and, with a son sinking down to death, he had nothing to lose in another attempt. It must have been with a mixture of dismay and hope that the man headed home to Capernaum. Jesus had declined to go with him, was not going to lay hands on his son, yet had spoken with assurance: "Go; your son will live" (4:50). Perhaps, the official must have thought, that would be enough.

If the official had an introspective bent at all, he knew how catastrophic illness can fragment one's faith. He knew, too, to what lengths one will go to hold on to hope and to try one more thing. He knew, as well, how frail our certainties become when we face a death in the family, especially the death of a child. What we have thought of as one whole (a picture of our lives and the people who surround it and the generations expected to come) begins to fragment and tear, like the tatters of brown, cracked photos in a family album. What we have thought of as a sure trajectory into the future (children growing up, going their unique ways, delighting our aging with grandchildren) suddenly veers into a dead end street. Then someone comes along who might do something. If that someone should give us nothing but a word of encouragement, we are left clutching the family pictures and heading home from God-knows-where without a map.

Desperate hope and shaky faith: that was what the official set out with. When the servants reached him on the road with the news that his son's fever had broken, his stomach unknotted. His determined walk slowed for a moment. We can surmise that soft tears flowed. Then a realization struck him. Whoever this Jesus was, he was able to reach and touch and alter from the center of his being. He had no mere premonition but a confident sense of how events would turn. Something in him arose with certitude from powers and realities the royal official barely knew.

The story, as we have it, never says that the royal official prayed. It merely says that he believed, and then his household with him. In what exactly they believed, they themselves perhaps hardly guessed, but they knew in whom they believed. Ready or not, the official had engaged in a last ditch effort that became a wide channel of personal faith.

God of life, help me believe even when I cannot sense your hands-on love. Give me confidence that you desire life and well-being for me and mine.

For Reflection

What sources of comfort, reassurance, and faith have I found in prayer, the sacraments, Scripture, and my church community? Is there anywhere else I have thought of turning?

Do I trust Julian of Norwich's certainty that "All shall be well and all shall be well and all manner of things shall be well"? Why or why not? How far do I go with hope?

Thirty-Eight Years Waiting

John 5:1–18

Now in Jersalem by the Sheep Gate there is a pool,
called in Hebrew Beth-zatha, which has five porticoes.
In these lay many invalids—blind, lame, and paralyzed.

The beloved disciple was stirred, like the pool called Beth-zatha, by the scene he witnessed near the Sheep Gate. God's healing seems to have taken place there for years. It was expected, with a village-simple mix of religious faith, superstition, and reliance on luck. Whoever got there first, they believed, would be healed. Getting there first required a virtual sprint at the first sign of the pool's stirring, at its first bubble or burst or spring. Ironic, since the competitors were the least able to see or sprint, and not all had someone to help them.

What the disciples saw was another Jerusalem interlude wherein Jesus broke through expectation, superstition, and taboo. He had pity on a weak, disabled man who had waited a long stretch of years to be first and to be made well. Jesus commanded him to take his straw mat in hand and to stand. In his sick wraps, the man stood, stunned by the command, startled that a healing strength overtook him without so much as a splash of water. He hardly had time to grasp the momentous reversal of his condition and the altogether new form of his life, when other forces beset him.

From sudden excitement and unexpected strength, he found himself cast immediately upon the incredulity and pettiness of the bystanders. He was reminded that carrying his mat constituted work forbidden on the Sabbath. He was treated to the derision of a carnival sideshow.

In the hasty onset of his healing, he realized that he had not asked the healer's name and now was unable to give an accounting of his transformation. He could not tell who had commanded him to stand up straight, whose voice was strong enough to overcome his doubt and pain, or where his new muscle and nerve had come from.

Later, after this man who was paralyzed for thirty-eight years had become slightly more accustomed to feeling the flex of his legs, the bend of his knees, the fall of his feet on pavement, he came upon the healer again in the temple precincts. They exchanged few words, but Jesus urged him to revel in his newfound health and to avoid sin. The man did no more than learn Jesus' name before he went off and made it known.

Jesus could only shrug. A straightened man must need some credibility with the authorities, even if they had never lifted a finger to help him or clear his way to the pool, even if they had never taken note of him until he took his mat in hand, stood erect, and began hauling it behind him. The authorities busied themselves with worrying over who the miracle worker might be and why he wasn't following their holy rules. They worried about a person who might influence someone to carry a mat on a non-workday.

Jesus shrugged again. The Creator works on behalf of well-being, he thought, even on a day of rest, so he would work, too. The man would have to decide whether to carry that mat or just drop it and leave it wherever it fell. "Do you want to be made well?" Jesus had asked him (5:6). Making good and making well seemed like Sabbath prayer.

Disciples and bystanders and former paralytics would have to learn this for themselves: what counted as work, as rest, as weal, as woe.

God of rising and uprising, stir my confidence so that I know where good is, when proscriptions and taboos no longer apply, and where well-being lies. Let me simply thank you for straightening my walk, telling me who you are, and strengthening my way.

For Reflection

The paralytic is pleased, even amazed and overjoyed, at his healing. Yet he is also a pleaser. What still needs to be healed in him? What in me? What might be five porticoes to healing for me? How do I understand the observance of the Christian Sabbath? Do I really observe it?

The Continuing Case of the Paralytic

John 5:19–30

"The Father judges no one but has given all judgment to the Son, so that all may honor the Son just as they honor the Father."

After the healing of the thirty-eight-year paralytic, conflict predictably ensued and grew. It was not so much the case of an inexplicable healing, or the fuss about whether Jesus had offended the heart of the Torah by working on the Sabbath and commanding another to work. No, it was more over the rumors that he was claiming a kind of equivalence with the Father. Once the paralytic had identified him, they knew that the healer was the very same itinerant rabbi who implied he had power over life, power over law, innate authority. To cap it off, he offended further by claiming the right to "judgment" and asserting that "honor" was due to him like the honor due to God. Such talk, in Jesus' day, would be enough to earn the charge of blasphemy. In our day, it would invite a diagnosis of megalomania. Here was a person who thought divinity was in his pocket. He pushed and pressed his claims, even arrogantly.

Yet the conflict, as the "beloved" recounts it, seems to have been about even more than that. After all, it was recorded by one of the disciples who had witnessed the rabbi's actions and words and had discussed their meaning with some of the other eleven. The disciples handed on this story, along with so many others, to a community and then to multiple communities, all of whose members remained unscathed and unscandalized by what must have seemed, at some point in their faith lives, inflated claims.

No, something else marked the escalating discomfort of those who wanted to bait, entrap, banish, and finally silence Jesus. He had just enough of a ring of truth about him. A winsome quality characterized his outrageousness. He was unsettlingly unimpressed with those who thought they had power, authority, the rights of earthly judgment, and a measure of control in the religious realm. He refused to take them seriously. He let it be known that he, apparently an unlettered man, not strictly observant, not a product of proper rabbinical schools, had spiritual prerogatives.

If Jesus could convincingly claim authority for himself, he could claim it for every son or daughter of humanity. Such a claim could deconstruct a system. It could usher in a reign of religious anarchy. To an already threatened people, it could sound as though the dismantling of every certainty and the demotion of every chosen soul was imminent.

They were afraid for their security as well as their certitudes. Aside from that, Jean Vanier suggests, they may have been afraid that their own strictures would be so loosened that others would get up and walk. Vanier says of this segment of the gospel: "Jesus is revealing that the healing of this paralyzed man is a sign of the presence and love of God, who wants to heal the inner paralysis in each one of us" (*Drawn into the Mystery of Jesus through the Gospel of John*, p. 113).

In the midst of splendid self-talk, Jesus seemed to be inviting the rabble to rise up and judge for themselves. Keeping some individuals crippled is far safer if one is resolved on maintaining things as they are. Jesus obviously had no such resolve.

God, teach me when to claim my human rights and trust that you speak and act through me. Let me hear my Brother speak for me when he speaks for himself, too.

For Reflection

What spiritual, rubrical, religious applecart am I zealously guarding from being upset? Does it ever seem to me that Jesus could be dangerous enough to ask me to help upset it?

Is there some paralysis of which I need to be set free? Do I ask or simply expect God to see and act?

The Things of This World

John 5:31–47 and John 6:1–5

"Not that I accept such human testimony,
but I say these things so that you may be saved."

Jesus set up a dialectic, a dynamism and tension in which those who observed him and knew him were caught. At times there were two poles that were absolute contradictories, at others, a creative struggle from which victory and truth could emerge. On one side were the values of the world, on the other, the purposes of the Father. On one side was the human brand of glory, on the other, the glory given freely and lavishly from heaven above. On the one side was the kind of truth humans might proclaim about themselves; on the other, were the testimony of Moses, the works of God, and the one whose voice has never been heard and whose form has never been seen (5:37).

Jesus made it clear that he disdained claims to worldly values, worldly glory, and worldly truth claims insofar as these are purely and restrictively secular. Such values, glory, and truth claims were narrow—and, he implied, typically self-centered and self-serving. Yet he did not hesitate to make some claims about himself—about his values (the works given him by the Father), about his glory (in that he would only accept glory from the Father), and about the testimony to truth that he bore (which, he noted, was greater than that of John the Baptizer). He renounced the world in its worldliness. At the same time, though, he walked in the world, addressed it, cited the Scriptures which it had recorded, and invited the world to "come to me to have life" (5:40).

Jesus was engaged in a delicate balancing act. He juggled the seen and the unseen, tossed up in the air the problems of the present even as he reached up to catch, like the juggler's whirling plate, eternal possibilities. All the while he was riding a unicycle on a high wire. Exasperated, he fired off the accusation that those around him could not possibly "have the love of God" within them (5:42), even as he begged and cajoled them to believe so that they could receive God's love.

So, right after denouncing the world and everyone who fell short in the realm of seeing, receiving, and believing (which seemed to be nearly everyone), Jesus crossed the Sea of Galilee. He then found himself involved in a very worldly worry about what the crowds would eat.

Lord of everything that is true, help me receive everything that testifies to you. Make my life a clearer, truer testimony.

For Reflection

Sometimes Jesus seems to want to shake the dust off everything. John narrates a number of such occasions. What do I see distressing Jesus? What made him seem so embittered against this world and its standards? What distress and bitterness do I expect he might feel even now?

How do I account for the fact that Jesus always comes back to our crazy world and renews his attentiveness to it?

The Bread of Forever

John 6:5–71

"Very truly, I tell you, whoever believes has eternal life. I am the bread of life."

It must have been a day the color of wheat. On such a day, especially if one is bedazzled by the sun, stretched taut with fatigue, and ready to yield to whatever offers respite and sleep, one can fancy himself or herself a firefly, a cornflower, a dust devil in the desert, a froth of high cloud. When the weight of cypress or the scent of pine seems enough to be a heaven, one may more easily receive a strange word.

On such a day Jesus decided to speak of himself as bread. The day before, the crowds had been hungry, for sure, and longing for the warm smells and sure solace of mother and home. The barley loaves and fish miraculously came and came and came. The next day they were hungry again and blind with the din and fatigue of multiplied food, storm at sea, and stalking crowds. Jesus then said: "I am the bread of life. Believe in me. Eat and live forever."

"And I'm Moses, or a night star, or a terebinth at Mamre," the most tired among them thought. "Now what? More riddles from the Master?"

Everything he said and did swiped at the sides of their heads. Yet he commanded attention.

"Consume me," he seemed to mean. "Remember, I am more than my mere visible self. You've seen the evidence already, repeatedly. You know our God, the manna-giver? That loving God has more to feed you with, through me. So eat me up. Drink me in. There will always be enough, and then some."

Thus it went. It played back in the people's sodden minds. All some of them wanted to do was to flop on the grass and clasp a rock for a pillow. All some of them wanted was today's morsels or repast, whatever it was to be. But Jesus would go cosmic on them and pummel them, like hailstones or cinders of asteroids, dropping with more and more of the same substance.

John watched with the others, wondering again what they had all been caught in.

The day was the color of wheat. The people squabbled among themselves about what Jesus could mean. Some scattered. Then Peter heaved a sigh. "Lord, to whom can we go?" he queried, as if any thought of an answer made him more tired (6:68). For Peter, the deep pause before the comment or question always meant the same thing: Act first, or at least concede. Understand later, if and when you can.

"I myself am bread." It would ring in John's ears forever, and play and replay, decade after decade, in the blessings shaped by his hands.

Bread of life and Lord of the universe, grant me wonder at the way you leave yourself behind and bring yourself to me and to all of us again and again. Give me reverence for your bread, your saving cup, your priestly people—for everything of you that is blessed and broken, blessed and shared, given once and again for all.

For Reflection

The church has fed on the Eucharist forever, even without altogether understanding. How do I explain to myself and to others what we believe about Mass, communion, and ourselves as eucharistic people?

Have I ever asked myself, the church, or God where else I would go? Presuming that I stay, how do I explain why?

A Eucharistic Interlude

John 6:63–65

"The words that I have spoken to you are spirit and life."

Despite its lack of ceremony, the bread of life sermon underlies all our liturgy. It was not about the conceptual, John knew. It was about believing with your whole body, with every sinew, every corpuscle, and all the salt in your sweat. Yet it was beyond that, never only flesh. It meant believing with your whole imagination, your deepest hope, your most profound daydream. "Spirit and life," Jesus had said.

In the memorials that arose later, after the ascension, after the descent of fire on the disciples, Spirit and life were always there—in the holy writ they read and the tales of Jesus they recollected, in the blessing and passing of loaf and cup, in the breaking into which they wholeheartedly went, side by side.

Diane Ackerman observes, in *Deep Play*, that absorbing games, human lovemaking, and religious ritual have a number of vital elements in common. They arise from and use the natural even while reshaping and ceremonializing it. They engage our senses and exalt them. They so concentrate our attention that workaday time frames fail to hold. They have their own rules, codes, signals, and gestures. They are expressive of and to some extent fulfill our longing for transcendence.

The sermon by Jesus and the actions of the Last Supper have all these elements of play, lovemaking, and formal worship. The

Eucharist offers us body to body contact, a unique language of consecration, and an offer of our own transformation into the Christ-life. The Eucharist draws us, from blessing over bread and words spoken over wine, to the divinizing of our own pulse beat and breath. We become more than the guests at a banquet or the consumers of fast food, more than the chefs in our family kitchens or the wait staff at the parish picnic. We become more than dieters or body-builders calculating food intake for our own special effects. Instead, we are offered to be offering, blessed to be blessing, and fed to be food for an emaciated world.

We are served bread, spirit, and life in an order of worship, a well-laid set of rubrics, a celebration overflowing with readings, vestments, responsories, and song. We are served an act of faith.

And Jesus knew, John could readily attest, that it is only in faith that we can play together, make love, and pray.

Spirit-giver and living bread, fill me with faith to hear, bless, take, eat, and be your body in this time, this place. Guide me in pouring myself out as wine for human thirst.

For Reflection

As a receiver of the Eucharist—repeatedly, for years—what famine of the spirit have I fed, and whose?

On Home Ground

John 7:1–9

After this Jesus went about in Galilee.

There is a Galilee of the soul. It is not the center of code or cult. It has no power center or court. The Galilee of the soul is noted for its crossroads and its roughnecks, its simple skills at weaving and casting out upon a small sea, its savvy at traversing desert, its comfort with proverbs, and folk wisdom, and an ease with Scripture that does not require a rabbinical school. This Galilee plies many crafts and teaches carpentry an attunement to the will of wood. It sweeps its house and welcomes guests without fuss and fanfare. This Galilee of the soul is simply down-home.

Robert Hamma reminds us, in *Landscapes of the Soul*, that the Galilee of Jesus, especially around the fertile Nazareth Valley, was and is a place where wild wheat and wild flowers grow, where grapevines and almonds abound, where cucumbers and garlic may be found, and where sheep can range the hills. Jesus must have found solace in the color and taste of his region and town. There he could sing to himself "All Is Well with My Soul" in whatever its contemporary version might have been. The Galilean small town, the Nazareth of the soul, especially around 30 C.E., was a spot where living came easy as long as there was rain. It was a homey town where color flashed from the ground. For the lover, for the beloved, for the family, for the circle of friends and faith, it was lovely and a bit off-road.

So Jesus' Galilee was a good place to cool down and a safe place to hide away for a while. Jesus knew that, as he determined not to hasten into the heartland of those who wanted to kill him. He sought there a simple and unceremonious Feast of Booths, a spot to pitch his tent as tents were being erected, a lean-to to lean on where he might purchase a pocket of flat bread. He wanted to hear the whistled tunes of his youth and the echoes of a long night's lullaby. "Let them all go on," he thought. "I'll stay home."

The Galilee of the soul is also a place for pacing when one begins to think that perhaps he or she needs to be somewhere else. And apparently, he began to pace.

God of my nostalgia and God of the child within me who always needs a safe and uncomplicated place, bring me to that soul center when I need it most. Let me be still there, just long enough.

For Reflection

Where is Galilee for me—a refuge place, a comforting home, a site for being still and regrouping? Do I, can I, sometimes go there? When and how?

The Wanderer's Song

John 7:10–36

But after his brothers had gone to the festival, then he also went, not publicly but as it were in secret.

There are melodies, children say, that get stuck in your head—for example, "Hey-Dum-Diddely-Dum," an old sea chanty. "Jesus, Remember Me," sung over and over at church, is another one. Children recall it from one Holy Week to the next. They break into the remembered song with energy. They enter into the hymn with a low hum. The words stay and the tunes hold. Grade four rollicks with the sea at the school performance night. Grades two through eight do Taize in church with a fall, a rise, and a final whisper. The songs call them back.

Ceremonies, memorials, and festivals do the same. After years of custom, it is hard not to participate in them.

Against his first impulse, Jesus headed to Jerusalem. Danger lurked and drama awaited him. In Chapter 7 of John's gospel, the word "kill" appears four times, two-thirds as many times as the word "Messiah." While threats encircled him, Jesus was saddened not to be where cult and custom were in an annual heydey. He needed to be where he usually would have been, among the pious, among God's chosen, in David's city, at Solomon's temple, even if his presence meant death.

At first, he went by stealth. By the middle of the festival, though, he could no longer refrain from speaking out and teaching. The people found him learned. They found him good. They found him messianic. And he made them nervous.

No one quite knew what Jesus was about, who had taught him, or who had sent him. Those who did know something, the ones who loved him, let him disclose only as much as he wanted to. They offered neither yea or nay when temple police went looking and when rumor was afoot that Jesus was going to the Greeks. All his followers knew was his name, where he was from, and the ring of truth that reverberated within them.

The watchers and listeners did not know, and would not for a while, the songs that were stuck in his head.

They were Hallel psalms. They were kaddish, too. They were songs of ascent and songs of lamentation and a song of two syllables: Abba. Jesus hummed. He sang to himself. The people began increasingly to overhear him.

Jesus, you change your mind and you chide. Sometimes you seem to goad me to rebellion. Let me simply trust that you know what you are about, even when I perceive that we—you and I—are on a seesaw ride. As we ride, let me join your song.

For Reflection

Jesus was nearly obsessed, according to the gospel of John, with his "hour." Several times it seems that he shifted position on the timing of things. How do you account for the not going-going shift, the secret-public shift, the readiness for arrest and the actual non-arrest? Did Jesus, in his humanity, always have the timing of eternity clear? If he didn't, how can I discern God's timing?

Living Spirit

John 7:37–52

"Out of the believer's heart shall flow rivers of living water." Now he said this about the Spirit, which believers in him were to receive; for as yet there was no Spirit.

In those early decades a Samaritan contingent to the community of believers clustered around the beloved disciple. At least, that is what the evidence suggests to Scripture scholar Raymond Brown, author of *The Community of the Beloved Disciple*. If that were so, they were familiar with the image of living water—and Christ's declaration that he offered it, poured it out, and refilled one's empty jugs and pitchers with it. The Samaritans had it first on the say-so of the woman at the well.

Then what? This community, it seems, believed with all its heart in the Christ and the Holy Spirit he imparted. They believed in baptism, bread of life, foot washing, and endless love. They trusted in the vine and branches and looked forward to what the sheepgate opened to. They were in the world but were beyond being entrapped by it. They eagerly anticipated another home in the world to come.

Meanwhile, what the disciples learned gradually, by experience and by contemplating this experience, was that the Paraclete had and did indeed come. The Spirit was in their midst guaranteeing truth and leading in love. They saw that they, too, imparted the Spirit as they let Christ's Spirit overtake them.

No, they were not orphans. They were not motherless or fatherless children. They were sisters and brothers in the Lord. They were midwives, physicians, and parents, too, bringing to birth the life of the Spirit in others. They were water-bearers, bringing the life in the Spirit home. They were weird comparison living in the here and now and wading into the world to come.

That was what the disciples knew by the time someone recorded Jesus' words.

Before that, though, there had been a time when they did not quite know that they could breathe on dry land, with the lungs the Lord had left them, a time when they did not know that they could inhale and exhale because of what their Love had left, the cooling, fierce power of God-breath.

Holy Spirit, inundate me yet again. Assure me that I know you; and may I let myself be so flooded that I, too, may impart you.

For Reflection

The Spirit forms us, forms community, forms all church everywhere. Why, then, do Scripture scholars put extraordinary emphasis on the Holy Spirit when they speculate about the Christian community or communities associated with the name of the apostle John? Are there parish or covenant communities today which seem to me especially marked as Spirited churches?

It is the Spirit, this passage implies, who opens eyes and opens minds. Without openness begotten of the Spirit one would never recognize the Messiah and never concede that God could summon a Messiah from Galilee. What openness of the Spirit may I now need to see more clearly how God is acting in my day?

Reading God's Heart

John 8:1–11

"Now in the law Moses commanded us to stone such women. Now what do you say?"

At the beginning of his gospel, John declares, "No one has ever seen God. It is God the only Son, who is close to the Father's heart, who has made him known" (1:18). One of the most stunning revelations of God's heart comes in Jesus' encounter with the woman caught in adultery. In this moment we see in our God empathy rather than enforcement, compassion rather than censure, gentle invitation rather than stern admonition.

God's heart was revealed to those who would see because of Jesus' own open, attentive heart. He was in the temple quietly teaching. Then suddenly a group of Pharisee roughnecks heaved a woman in and interrupted him: "See! Caught in the act! So what will you do?" They baited him, pitting him, as they saw it, against Moses and long legal tradition. They already knew, obviously, his habitual acceptance of people on their own terms, his forbearance, his reluctance to use even harsh language, much less harsh action. They practically tossed her toward him. We can picture her, a loose wrapping of garments hastily thrown on, terror in her eyes, and then the empty look of the helpless. A lover by stealth and by night, she had been dragged in alone.

Jesus avoided looking directly at her in that state, amid the press of listeners and ruffians. Instead, he took a deep breath and bent down. He began tracing on the ground. Students of Semitic culture tell us that doodling in the dust is a classic and pointed expression of supreme boredom. Then he leveled the challenge: "Let anyone among you who is without sin be the first to throw a stone at her" (8:7). Suddenly there was an even match: no side of virtue opposed by the side of vice, no side of justice opposed by the side of crime. It was simply a question. Who has never transgressed? Who has the right to condemn?

When they all left, beginning with those who had had the most time to accumulate error and sin, he finally faced her squarely. "Woman," he called her, using the same address he applied to his mother. With feigned shock, he asked if anyone had stayed on to condemn her. As she replied, "No," the quaver in her voice turned to sheer astonishment. And so he said that he would not condemn her either. Then, urging her to go, he quietly cautioned her to avoid future sin. We can picture her clutching her robe around her, planting her sandals in the dust with shaken yet steadier footfall.

Whatever else Jesus had done here, at his own risk, he had offered a balm of comfort and gentle breeze. "God knows," he may as well have said. There were many sins besides sins of the flesh, and passionate love could not be counted the worst. "Learn first to do no harm," he must have mused to himself. For it was clearly sin to reduce a human to a trial run or plaything. And that was exactly what the crowd had done. So he composed this sermon in his head for those who had fled. "Before you grasp stones in your fist and get set to fling them, recall you own sad errors, your share in fruitless search."

Jesus never said these words, nor were they inscribed in any text. John may have read them there, though, in the rabbi's eyes. And there he had read, too, God's heart.

Let me come before you, Lord, confident that you love me in my pain, and read my hungry, hurting heart.

For Reflection

When have I been the condemning Pharisee? When the caught woman? When the embodiment of the Father's tender heart?

Light to the Left, Light to the Right

John 8:12–33

"Even if I testify on my own behalf, my testimony is valid because I know where I have come from and where I am going."

In the tense aftermath of the episode with the woman caught in adultery, amid high stress hours when Jesus must still have wondered whether it would have been wiser to stay in Nazareth, Jesus spoke of lasting light and inner authority.

I think of the light off the South Carolina coast. From the fishing pier at Folly Beach, one first sees daylight off to the left. The eastern sky breaks into streams of dawn's pastels. But the sky above the sea-line is never utterly dark, not even at the vanishing point of the moon. Morris Island lighthouse stands offshore there, splaying shafts of yellow amid breakers and dark wind, or in the calm and cloudless sky. The light simply lasts. Off to the right, too, there is light. After the last west dip of sun, after the yellow and pink fade to purple-gray and blue-black, the light of a channel marker and a steadied boat shine, at 8:00, then at 9:00, at night.

There is some light source, he promised, some guiding. For the one who will look, left and right, there will always be, Jesus seemed to say, enough light. What credence, though, could they give him? Why take note at all of his assurances and claims?

The beloved disciple and the others saw Jesus rebuke those who would doubt his veracity. He did it this way, then that. During the days of the Feast of Booths, he simply asserted his inner authority.

He had a mission, he knew who he was, he knew his origin, he knew his destination, he knew that he bore goodness, he knew he could trust his own impulses and insights, he knew that everything was about truth and timing. He required no letters of recommendation, no background checks, no citations of endless reputable sources. Jesus did not need back-up.

He flabbergasted them, though, with his reason why: He trusted his own inner authority, and he felt the validation of the Father. He was unashamed to claim them, with astounding confidence.

In the end perhaps they hated him for what seemed an arrogant lack of humility or self-deprecation. Perhaps they hated him for being so sure of things and for his proclivity for reaching as high as heaven. He spoke familiarly of the God from whom he said he had come—the very God to whom they bowed, about whom they philosophized, of whom they wondered what pure Being might be.

That blithe familiarity filled them with consternation, even as it eased the unlettered, the less confident, the timid, and the invalidated into his embrace—even as it lit their way.

Giver of purpose and voice, color my skies by day and light my way by night. Help me give over to your authority and to speak, stride, and season my life with you.

For Reflection

"Why do I speak to you at all?" an exasperated Jesus exclaimed (8:25), when it seemed the scribes and Pharisees had missed everything. They acted as though they had no notion of who he might be, why he was speaking to them, what he might mean. We can picture them as the three monkeys with ears, eyes, and mouths covered respectively. Can I imagine times when I appear dense to Jesus? Am I dense deliberately?

"You will know the truth, and the truth will make you free" (8:31). Are there times I would prefer to be in the dark? Are there some freedoms that frighten me? In what areas of my life might I lack freedom? How does this keep me from holiness and happiness?

The Weaving of Thorns

John 8:34–59

"Are we not right in saying that you are
a Samaritan and have a demon?"

Those who are in love come to see with new eyes. The brilliance of sky and stream suddenly become dazzling. Splashes of autumn color become the fireworks of the mountains. The cooler in the grocery store, never noticed before, overflows with flowers. All the world looks beautiful. The faces and fabrics and fuming buses and frantic taxis of New York's Fifth Avenue are new and vibrant life-signs. Whiskers on the face and even the scent of sweat awaken the heart. Knockout loveliness blooms and scatters all about.

So what of pain and the world's disdain? If the lover is sensitized to what is wondrous, she or he can assuredly be more deeply offended by what denies life, belittles persons, or brutalizes. The beloved disciple knew and was horrified. The wisest and most loving man could be misunderstood and reviled. The most exquisite of lovers could be pursued as if he were a solicitor of child sex and a purveyor of the most dire sadness. The most truthful of teachers, a prince among men, could be shunned and spat upon as if he were a traitor who had undone his nation. They prejudged him as they did their natural enemy and favorite scapegoat, the Samaritan. They demonized him. They derided his references to Abraham. When Jesus affirmed, "Before Abraham was, I am," they grabbed at stones to fling at him, as hard as they could.

It made no sense and makes none today. The best and the most beautiful appear in bounty, and slime is summoned to engulf them. That is what the beloved disciple saw. Pure love was being encircled as a slow crown of thorns was being woven.

There is a sickness that even roses can come to. It made John world-weary and left him bereft of explanation. The rabbi spoke of glory. All around him were persecutors and plotters. How could God's word and work come to such grief?

I wonder, too, God, how can your creation and all who image you on earth come to grief? Why do we shun, mock, prejudge, and kill? Why do we turn good inside out until the bouquet of love and the rose of hope wilt, spot with blight, and fall away, a petal at a time? Why can I only ask what "we" do rather than lay claim to the grief I engineer, the damage I do?

For Reflection

Jesus attested that he had been sent by God, and he laid claim to foreknowledge of prophecies and patriarchs. How do I understand the interaction of Jesus' humanity and his divinity as he tries both to understand and to make understood his own mission?

The Blind, the Sinful

John 9:1–41

"Rabbi, who sinned, this man or his parents, that he was born blind?"

If ever there was someone who had been batted around, it is the blind man whose story is told by John. In his day, in his hour, he rapidly became the object of questions and sick-soul theology. If something had gone wrong, it must have been someone's fault. It must have been a punishment. Jesus had amply sidestepped such thinking, but it persisted in his disciples anyway. So, he dismissed it. No, a man isn't born blind because of personal sin—not his own, on some strange backfire to conception; not his parents, displaced like the rage that whacks children and kicks dogs. Jesus simply suggests that there is something to be learned from his actions, something about God's works.

What Jesus had done to the blind man was to touch him, to salve mud on his eyes, to tell him to wash. Thus the man had begun to see for the first time.

The blind man, meanwhile, barely knew what had gone on. He could not say what Jesus looked like. His eyes, after all, were unaccustomed to seeing. He knew the voice, however, and the name. He knew the rabbi's touch, too—truly. And so, all that he could say of Jesus, who continued to irritate people with his Sabbath ventures, was, "He is a prophet" (9:17).

The newly-sighted man's parents batted him around, too. We get the feeling, from his initial isolation, that the blind son had been an embarrassment. Some years back, they apparently had distanced him from themselves. "He's of age," they said, dodging pharisaical questions. "He will speak for himself," they insisted, reiterating their separateness from him and his plight. They were afraid, certainly, of guilt by association with a disabled son and a mad messiah. They had been steeped in fear all their lives, it would seem.

The son spoke for himself, though, and clothed himself in the dignity of knowing that the power to heal the blind was no small thing. It had to be of God. Of this he was certain. Evil would not relieve suffering. Malevolence could not act to make whole. And so the questioners dismissed him.

Then Jesus sought him out. He told the man that he had seen not just the light of day, not just his parents' faces and their cowardice, not just the hatred seething in certain human hearts. He had also seen the Son of Man, Jesus assured him. And so the blind man believed.

Sin had no part of his story. Except for the sin of ashamed parents. Except for the sin of the rabble who thought themselves stubbornly religious and capable of pointing to an explanation for everything. Except for the sin of the disciples who saw an object lesson rather than a human being. Jesus had seen a lonely man, a man reduced to beggary, but a man with light within. He determined to make bright light of this man, touching him, freeing him, seeking him once again, counseling with him. He reshaped the man with mud, as though he were some fine, upright, elect Adam.

Jesus found a blind man. In a matter of moments and prayer, a seeing man fell on his knees as he never had. He would kneel no more to anyone but his God.

God of light, touch me so that light within illumines me. Shape me into the dignity of a firstborn and favored. Then let me worship and go free.

For Reflection

What is it about us that demands an explanation for innocent suffering? Why do we find it so hard to accept the innocence of the sufferer? What blindness should I ask to be healed of?

The Shepherd, the World

John 10:1–21

"He calls his own sheep by name and leads them out."

It was Rudolph Bultmann who first noted the possibility of dividing the Gospel of John into halves: "Revelation of Glory before the World" (chapters 1–12) and "Revelation of Glory to the Congregation" (chapters 13–20). The passages about the sheepgate and the good shepherd, while in the "world" section (in Bultmann's schema, presented in D. Moody Smith, *The Theology of the Gospel of John*, pp. 20–21) seem to anticipate the move specifically toward revelation to the community—and even separation into it.

One of the movements which the beloved disciple perceived was in-gathering. Despite all the public, and indeed widespread, forays of Jesus and his proclamations—at Cana, in Judea, into Samaria, at the wedding feast, well-side and lakeside, in the temple precincts, and on dusty roads—there is a drawing in that gathers disciples and friends, "closens" them, if we may coin such a term.

Since one of the pressures on what has been called the Johannine community was hostility toward them on the part of traditional Judaism and "the world" in general, it isn't surprising to find the disciple having to speak, at times, words of assurance, security, and stability. He recalled Jesus calling himself sheepgate and shepherd, both entry way and protector of "the fold." What might that show? Jesus' personifying the gate and identifying himself with it was a sign that he was reliable; he was himself a hostel, a safe-house.

Their compound was guarded by one who loved the vulnerable. In speaking of himself as shepherd, Jesus again adopted the posture of guide and protector. As D. Moody Smith has noted: "He presents himself as both the door of the sheep (verse 7) and the good shepherd (verse 11), and although the switch in imagery may be confusing, the centrality of Jesus and his loyalty to the flock are clear. Other shadowy figures, the thieves and robbers, the stranger, the hireling, and the wolf obviously represent those who would mislead, abandon, or attack the sheep.... Followers of Jesus appear as people threatened, but Jesus is their protector" (Smith, p. 33).

In a world of dynamic opposites and sometimes of dangerous contradictions, Jesus presented himself as helper and hero, strong man and gentle shepherd, safeguarder, and caregiver to his embattled disciples. The image of good shepherd, which has comforted people for millennia, says to the community that they can count on being herded, headed, and carried when necessary. What Jesus wanted—and it is the essence of shalom—was and is to give confident assurance to the faithful that they will not be left alone. Jesus will lead the flock "in and out," he pledged (10:9). His voice will strengthen and succor. His footfall will make the path to pasture. What he wanted for them and wants for us is life "abundantly" (10:10). The disciple knew, in his sheepish bones, that the shepherd would even die to save the sheep.

Lord, your words of encouragement and strength have comforted believers for century upon century. Why, then, do I squirm—and sometimes go the way of the lost sheep? Bring me home, by hook or crook.

For Reflection

The images of sheepgate and shepherd are far less vivid for us today than they were for the hearers of the gospel in the first century of Christianity. What contemporary images might communicate the same truths of Jesus' love for his church and for each individual soul?

The Vagrant

John 10:22–39

"I give them eternal life, and they will never perish.
No one will snatch them out of my hand."

Adoration chapels and wide-open churches can be magnets for the dissolute and eccentric. People sometimes curl into a bow on the floor, their heads tucked under the curl, which unrolls to reveal stocking feet. An unshod, unsocked man who sports a beard and wears the same white robe each day comes for several months to Blessed Sacrament, Charleston, and washes there most evenings in its lavatory. One can hear him at the back of the chapel. Then he sits, still, rapt in prayer. A young man named Donnie, claiming to be a college student short of cash after midterms, pleads for $4.75 and is surprised when a nun gives him $5.00. His perspiration and backpack tell nothing of whether his plea for fare to Mount Pleasant is truth or lie. A man with cerebral palsy comes, and an older man clattering his walker, edging into the pew after his tired daughter has dropped him off and left. A sixty-something year-old bearded man in a T-shirt sits by his old mother who insists on coming, even though she no longer remembers why. A teenage girl slithers in and seems, behind straggly hair, to cry lightly. A middle-aged woman, struggling with unrelieved illness, fidgets and leaves, only to fight with one who loves her best.

Jesus told the beloved and people like the ones at Blessed Sacrament at night that they had won God's heart, everlastingly.

Trouble came, and threats of stoning, because he presumed to speak for God—"You, though only a human being," they taunted him (10:33).

His point was that God meant for all of them and all of us, the rabble, to be raised. Theosis, the Greeks called it; deification or divinization, the Latins. As Jesus saw it, God-likeness was and is our common destiny. Scripture, he noted, called "gods" those to whom God's word came (10:35). Why not?

There must be a God-self lurking within each and every one.

There was, he saw, as he studied the faces that winter, around and about the Feast of Dedication. There was, he noticed, as he watched who loitered and lingered around the temple, stealing a brief peace there. There were God-selves wriggling beneath those visages and just under their ordinary skin.

No one knows for sure when or if the Jesus-man in Charleston will ever come back. No one can tell whether Donnie will ever deliver the promised DVD for the sisters to watch. No one knows who, or if anyone, will pay forward what they've found in Solomon's portico or in a side chapel where a monstrance glows gold around the clock. Whatever becomes of them all, Jesus pledged that nothing good found by the wayfarers would ever be repossessed on them.

There was and is some God-stuff going on.

Whatever Godliness there is, Lord, within me, let it bubble up and through my dissoluteness and oddity.

For Reflection

What draws the lonely, the befuddled, and the broken to holy places? Have I ever seen myself in them? Have I envied their holy strangeness? Do I see God lingering within, awaiting my notice?

Broken Faith, Saved Faith

John 10:40–42

And many believed in him there.

Sandra Schneiders, in an early book about religious life, *New Wineskins*, used the gospel of John as the centerpiece of her discussion about commitment. What happened in the time of the beloved disciple, she proposes, may happen still. People may find themselves disengaging from institutional commitments, even religious ones, for the sake of a compelling new commitment. The disciples of the beloved disciple, for example, were essentially forced out of practical Judaism, denied entry to the synagogues, regarded as apostates, as defilers and defiers of Mosaic law. They were thought to have been making a god of a man—and a crucified criminal at that. One by one and as a group, they were driven to a hard choice: continue the privileges of temple, scroll, law, and prophets, and abandon "the Way," or continue on with the followers of the one they called the Christ, with their growing cadre of Gentiles and religious reprobates—and consider themselves excommunicated from the Chosen People.

Schneiders says the breaking of the prior commitment, the one to temple Judaism, was driven by an even more fundamental one: the commitment to truth, ultimate truth, as it resonated within, sounding the depths of the soul. Samaritans, blind men, adulteresses, Pharisees like Nicodemus, roustabout fishermen like Peter, impressionable youths like John, undistinguished homebodies like Martha found life-meaning, heart-resonance, and soul-longing fulfilled in Jesus. Even their old-time religion couldn't keep them from him.

Sometimes, Schneiders says, the press of God-truth and the demands of God-love unattach us and reattach us elsewhere. It happens when we find ourselves home.

For the beloved disciple and for his company, home was a person. Once upon a short time, he had crisscrossed their holy land and remained. They could not help but remain with him, forever after.

When, God, do I stay, and when do I go? How do I know? Direct my heart-search and lure me to your love-truth. Hold me close, if I need to let go of what was. Hold me tighter still as I grasp at what comes next. As you will.

For Reflection

Fidelity is a celebrated virtue, and loyalty is expected among those who have made bonds, pledged faith. When, to what, or in response to whom, might I find myself impelled to be what might be thought "infidel"? Do I have the courage to break faith when deeper faith compels me?

What examples come to mind of those who have broken a commitment to give themselves over to a deeper, holier call?

Unbinding

John 11:1–44

"But even now I know that God will give you whatever you ask."

Martha, without a doubt, adored Jesus. She ran first to meet him as he approached Bethany. She adored him, even though he had chided her (according to other evangelists) for her fussbudget ways around the house. She adored him, and she chided him, too: "If you had been here, my brother would not have died" (11:21). But she was quick to add the confidence: Even now, you can do something (11:22).

The relationship is hard to read. It was at her house, their house—Mary's and Lazarus' too—that Jesus came with unwashed feet whenever he needed to stretch out on a couch. Bystanders who knew all of them described his feeling for the family as love. Yet, bafflingly, he stalled returning when Martha summoned him, and he coolly said he was using what was going on as a lesson. Yet again, when he got there and faced the power-packed emotion of the two sisters, their dismay and grief at their brother's sudden death and their bewilderment at Jesus' inaction, he wept. Twice in the story it says that Jesus was "greatly disturbed." What were they to make of this friend? He cared and hesitated. He was ready for drama but paused to test Martha's faith. He knew his power but was reluctant to use its full force. Life and death were in his hands, he seemed to know with assurance, yet he teetered on the edge of dropping his command as though it were a searing ka-bob skewer.

Approaching Jerusalem so closely was dangerous for him, Thomas and the others knew. Perhaps that is part of the explanation for his quick emotion and his prior hesitation. Then again, some of his seesaw about what to prioritize—mission and message or compassion and closeness—must have been the sheer tension of deep friendship. Some hurt must be endured, he must have mused. Moments of incapacity and moments of protracted response happen in every friendship or love. They come of human finitude. Jesus, though divine, lived his humanity fully and was subject to the fits and starts of sickness and health, time and the tug of death, travel weariness and the desire for an ordinary life. With the disciples, Jesus was resolute, certain, prepared to dramatize another evidence of God's reign. With Martha and then Mary, though, he was pained, stressed, and unnerved by the possibility that he had waited too long and caused affliction by his waiting.

When his confidence returned, though—as it quickly did—he took command. He called upon the Father in heaven with clarity and the conviction that all he asked would happen. He invoked the crowd's need for convincing. He ordered Lazarus back to life, unbound, freed.

Martha adored him, as did Mary, for every unbinding he had ever done. He had, after all, unbound them all for months and maybe years. He had unbound them even from the dread of death and its finality.

Like John, Lord, let me watch these scenes where Godhead and manhood pull you, press you, define you. Under every tension and every act, let me know the friend in you who weeps also for me.

For Reflection

What tensions and hesitations cause me at times to wonder which comes first—important tasks or beloved persons? How do I resolve these tensions?

What, in times of grief and funeral liturgies, gives me assurance that death has no final power? How do I understand Jesus' presence in the death of a loved one?

In Hiding and Then

John 11:45–57

Jesus therefore no longer walked about openly…
but went from there to a town called Ephraim in the region
near the wilderness; and he remained there with the disciples.

Where he went became a hideout and a holding pen. But deep down, the disciples knew that nothing could keep him away from the masses of people or the mysteries of Pesach. The festival drew him, not for its own sake, but because Jerusalem was the holy hill, the place of his consecration, the priestly citadel, the site where the story of liberation was enacted over and over. Passover in Jerusalem epitomized and sanctioned Passover in every Jewish home. The reenactment and renaming of God's action through Moses for Israel fired him. The retelling of redemption for a people poised to walk, with blood on the lintels of the hovels of their leavetaking, brought home again his mission. There was always a time for setting free. It was his mission as rabbi to clear their minds and untie their doubts. It was his mission as prophet to blaze the way and dislodge the stumbling blocks. It was his call as savior and Son to offer himself freely to bad will and fate so that final good might come.

Meanwhile, there was an interlude in Ephraim, a safety they could recall, a solitude they would hark back to when chaos descended. They enjoyed a closeness to him to which they would wish to cling.

Take me apart, Lord, with you, even if only for a short time. Strengthen me for what is to come. Free me enough that I may relish your freedom beckoning me.

For Reflection

When do I want to hide from responsibility or conflict or the next thing that will come at me? When do I need to?

The Anointing

John 12:1–11

Mary took a pound of costly perfume made of pure nard,
anointed Jesus' feet, and wiped them with her hair.

Why do we cry?
Because we are lonely.
Because someone we have loved has died.
Because we are afraid.
Because we are filled with regret.
Because no one sees as we do.
Because poverty gnaws at our hope
  and turns our children into pot-bellied stick figures.
Because we are tired unto death of pain.
Because plots and death-threats abound,
  even where we least expect.
Because the innocent suffer.
Because sin gets the best of us, or seems to.
Because often the good die young.
Because all we've dreamed and worked for
  can be whisked away as if we never were.

A soul friend loosened her hair and poured out a fortune in perfume. A dissolute disciple complained about a world of waste. A legendary housekeeper served her guests. A formerly dead man ate. Crowds came. Chief priests plotted—one murder, then two.

We, looking on from twenty-one centuries' distance, still don't know what to make of it all.

Something was afoot. Sanctity and the sinister met, with the sinister slowing the drumbeat of success down to a death march.

Jesus continued to eat. He told them to let things and persons be. For the moment, crying ceased. Perfume filled the room and an hour of peace.

God above, some days have been, some days will be, six days before the Passover of my life, too. There have been and will be days of disgruntlement and days of wild extravagance, days of sourness and days of food and drink. There are doomsday hours and moments of sheer tranquility. Give me, when I most need it, costly perfume and forgetfulness of anything but your aliveness, here and now.

For Reflection

When do I sense a need for respite before challenge? Where do I see God in others' gift-giving or extravagance?

Greek Sight-Seers

John 12:12–26

They came to Philip, who was from Bethsaida in Galilee, and said to him, "Sir, we wish to see Jesus."

Among the worshippers were Greeks, a minority among believers in the law, prophets, and festivals. It was their Passover, too, however, and there they were.

They knew the word "Hosanna." They knew the psalm from which "Blessed is he who comes in the name of the Lord" originated (118:26). They knew enough of the minor prophets to recall Zephaniah's heralding of the king of Israel in their midst (Zep 3:15). And if they thought about it, they might recall a "Rejoice!" from Zechariah that spoke of a king entering the city "humble and on a donkey" (Zec 9:9). What they might not have wanted to hear, though, was a reminder that grains of wheat must go down, be ground into soil, pass into darkness, cease aspiration before they could bear fruit. What they might not have wanted to recall was that crowds could turn—on anyone.

The Greeks who wanted to see him, were fringe worshippers, Jewish Greeks, an aberration, as far as some were concerned. They did not know what the connection might be between Jesus and Moses, prophecy, the coming reign of a promised messiah. They did not know whether anyone would care what they, who always felt like outsiders even though they were partially in, might come to believe. But they wanted to see Jesus anyway.

Come what may, they were there—somewhat displaced persons, somehow always just a bit out of step. Always off in their accent; always a bit less than proficient.

They did not know what he would think of them. But they wanted, deep down, to know what they themselves might think of him.

Even if he would never be their king as entirely as he might be for nearly everyone else in Jerusalem.

Sometimes, Lord, in the midst of everyone and everything, I feel irredeemably out of sync. I lack pedigree, propriety, and the neat fit. Entertain my desire for you, in spite of my lack. Humor me. And let me see for myself how I fit with you.

For Reflection

In church and society there are those who are estranged even while they are members. Who are they? Why might they feel that way? How have they come to feel that way?

What do we have to do with them?

Light Source

John 12:27–50

"While you have the light, believe in the light, so that you may become children of light."

One of the great difficulties about human potential movements, self-help books, and actualization workshops is that they acknowledge a great truth but typically fail to follow it to its source. There is more to us, they claim. There is power, unused capacity, an inner leader, a wisdom deep in the heart, a special You, a special Me yearning to be free and to hoot and holler. There is a magnetic personality just waiting for its appropriate atomic particles to veer north.

One work of this genre that comes close to the real deep source (aside from Laurie Beth Jones' *Jesus CEO* and John Maxwell's *Attitude 101*, *Leadership 101*, and so on) is Robert K. Cooper's *The Other 90%*. Cooper emphasizes that the making and doing of something meaningful in one's life is ultimately a matter of decision. One does or doesn't; one will or won't. If a person commits to a great cause, a worthy task, an authentic focus, he or she is led inevitably to a choice to live or not live. If it is to live, it must be with integrity. This takes a compelling purpose, though.

Cooper tells the story of the generations of Stevensons before Robert Louis who built and manned (and sometimes womanned) lighthouses. Guarding the Scottish coast seemed to them a worthy and even lifesaving task. It was worth devoting inventiveness and perseverance to. The lighthouse keepers endured daily inconvenience and, in some treacherous seasons, great personal pain. They faced isolation and the risk of frostbite, dark and storm and battering. The payoff, however, was due to the fidelity of the lighthouse keepers to their routine, to their sometimes monotonous, sometimes grueling efforts. Ships didn't founder. The lost could steer when there were no stars. Those adrift found the shore. The light, when they spotted it, beaconed them on.

Jesus urged, coaxed, invited, and cajoled his followers, assuring them that they could benefit from light and actually become it. He himself was and could be source and keeper. It meant, though, that he had not only to bear the fire but to stand in it. He had to endure the harshness of night and the drama of death. Yet his light shone on.

Only one thing frustrated Jesus: that there were some pilots, dull of sense and stubborn of soul, who would not look beyond the gloom. There were some who would not even acknowledge that a light had appeared somewhere off starboard because they thought the only world was the other side: port.

They missed the tinder, the mirrored height, the stream of light to their human potential, and they never caught sight. In the end, it was they who died, not he. Not the beacon. Not the bearer and keeper of living, golden beams.

Lord Jesus, light-maker, light-bearer, and lighthouse keeper, train my eye to see. I wait with you, who light me to the steady shore and harbor home of eternity.

For Reflection

What do I know of lighthouse lore and rescues at sea? Does the image of a spiritual lighthouse shine for me?

If I were to write, say, three key points for a self-help book, what advice for self-actualization would I give, based on my faith?

Footwashing

John 13:1–20

"You also should do as I have done to you."

A freeing moment comes. A diabetic, sick of safety and everlasting regimen, unstraps her shoes, yanks off her socks, and lets her toes and feet sink into the beach. There is something about hiking the pants legs higher and higher and getting wet past the knees. There is something about the pull of a slight undertow as wave after wave recedes, and the heels dig into wet sand.

So often those who have pondered the footwashing of Maundy Thursday have fixed their attention on Jesus, his self-abnegation, his example of abject servanthood, his secure non-assertion of his power and rightful role. They have commended the nurse who derives a sense of benefaction from her podiatry. They admire the way she has put the elderly, the disabled, and the mildly impaired on surer footing while she sits open-lapped and servant. They have mentioned all those whose hospitality not only shows no breach of etiquette but also lavish care on the guest. They have commended the leader, the administrator, the director who rolls up her or his sleeves and slogs the wet mop, paints the ceiling, heaves a pick, and washes the pots.

What the commentators and commenders miss, however, is the pleasure of the receiver. Attentive parents wash between the toes of their children's feet. Lovers massage and caress one another's feet out of the simple desire to relax one another. Friends spray faucets' worth and hose down each others' sandy feet at the beach. It feels good, plainly, to be touched and toweled. It slows every hectic and rattling inner thing down.

Jesus washed the disciples' feet. For a time they sank as into the pleasure of wet sand and the clear stream of breakers that tugs every lock of seaweed off.

On the night before his greatest pain, Jesus bestowed pleasure. That was something, perhaps, of what he meant for those who followed him to pass on.

Lord, I have longed to bare my feet and not to care if splinter or shard of glass slips in. For all I want is soft sand and rush of foam upon me, skin to skin. I thank you for the touch of your services and ask that you will free me enough that I may take deeper pleasure in them.

For Reflection

Why is it that we Christians speak so rarely of the joys that come from being the recipient? Are we perhaps lopsided in our celebration of giving?

Night

John 13:21–30

And it was night.

Night. Aside from the occasional "Hallelujah!" or the one-time "Maranatha!" this sentence declaring the arrival of Holy Thursday night is probably the shortest in Sacred Scripture. It is certainly one of the most dire.

Judas was about his treacherous business, and Jesus knew it. He had just confided his uneasiness and his premonition of imminent betrayal to the beloved disciple. He steeled himself and tried to steel his men, but Jesus was still beset by a sense of dread, and his dread washed over John and Peter. All was not well.

Some movements into night are tender. Moon touches leaves, and the leaves softly shift and fan in night breeze. The moon and stars are enwrapped in black and charcoal cloud while they remain outlined in blue light. Certainly not a douse but rather a dewdrop of damp cools the one who sits. On such nights love poems begin to be born as a line, an image, a tracing of wonder, a sigh going up.

Other forays into night are criminal. Thieves ransack house and vacant work-place in the shadows. Knives are raised from cloaks, and a swift glint and thrust flash blood from the unwary victim. Storms steal across the night sky, and the muffled drums of war blare suddenly into a sneak attack, and bombs fall.

Jesus' night was so mixed. Holy Thursday was a night of wine and remembrance. It was bread broken into eternal love poem. It was body and blood, among twelve bonded to God.

Yet the other side of night was gathering here, as dark and dissonance sank in. It was the gradual but deliberate mustering of Sanhedrin and imperial guard. It was the first several steps of a death march. A young man who had clothed himself for a religious feast, another gospel writer tells us, would shortly drop those very clothes in fear and flee. The first of the apostles, earlier attentive and conversing facilely, would draw a sword and mutilate a servant's ear. Wild panic would overtake the weary celebrants of that last meal with Jesus. Judas, heading off for traitorous work, would soon take his coins, the payoff, and fling them back as if it had all been massive misunderstanding. A man very much still alive yet very mistaken, Judas would tie himself with rope and drop from a tree in a hasty final act.

Darkness fell, and it would call for torches just so faces could be read in a still, quiet garden. A weight of dust and ash, unsuspected as those at supper reclined, would soon eat into the cells and interstices of lungs and heart—of one, of three, of many.

Worst of all, in the aftermath of holy recollection and prayer, there would seem to be a disappearance, a nowhereness, of God. And so, another would later tell, the Son who smiled and blessed, then tensed and whispered, would, before it was all over, sweat blood.

Meanwhile, they spoke softly and ate.

Assuredly, it was night.

Lord Jesus, lover and loser, teach me to wait through seeming hopelessness. Help me to live on in the dark and to hang on to your damp cloak. Let me stare down the dark squarely—with faith.

For Reflection

How do a few holy hours, the hours of adoration until midnight, in churches that have celebrated the Lord's Supper, help me relive this night? How do I locate Eucharist in the midst of conspiracy?

The Demands of Love

John 13:31–38

"By this everyone will know that you are my disciples, if you have love for one another."

They may not have known where he was going, and they may not have understood how his sense of mission and glory (*shekinah*) differed from theirs. They may not have understood why on this night, in particular, he called them "little children" or why he predicted the moral failure of one of them, Simon, his right-hand man and rock. They may perhaps have begun to grasp, though, what his command of love might mean and how even the feeblest attempt at obedience and implementation of love's demands would change them.

It would not be good enough, if they took him seriously, for them to live in mere peaceful coexistence with anyone. It would not satisfy if they simply became skilled at "tolerance."

Mother Teresa of Calcutta told and retold the stories of her sisters' ministry and its manner of fulfilling the commandment of love. She related an encounter with an abandoned and emaciated man who was washed, given clean nightclothes, and laid in a hospital bed, who exclaimed to her, "Mother, I have lived like an animal and you are helping me die like an angel." She recounted the story of a day when her sisters literally wrenched a man free from a streaming gutter where he lay at risk of being washed into an open drain. When they got the weak and broken man to their house of care, the sisters had to pick maggots from his body before they could even cleanse or change him. They did so with care. Why? Mother reminded them, faced with the horrendous sight and stench, that they were "picking maggots from the Body of Christ."

To sustain such love, a person needs a power source. A charismatic leader—a Mother Teresa of Calcutta, or her master, Jesus of Nazareth—helps and impels, of course. But that personal touch of inspiration and of bonded commitment to one another is also needful. The Missionaries of Charity live and sustain their love by hours of prayer—devotional, eucharistic, meditative, scriptural. They toughen themselves by living with far fewer than the typical creature comforts and, in fact, with some purposeful discomforts. They soften themselves, though, by listening to Mother's words, now remembered; to Sister Nirmala, their new superior; to one another; and, most searingly, to the cries of the poor. They bond for a cause, smile for a sufferer, and go it all together.

Those at table with Jesus would learn that and pass it on until it bore the weight of spiritual tradition and the very definition of God.

Lord, it is a plain and simple challenge and yet the most difficult of all: love other persons, wholeheartedly and unreservedly. Teach me how. Toughen me as I need, soften me in your way.

For Reflection

Dorothy Day, quoting Dostoevsky, remarked with some frequency that "love in action is a harsh and dreadful thing" compared to "love in dreams." When have I found myself loving till it hurts? Can I see myself ever being called to love in the mode of soup kitchen or homeless shelter host? Why or why not? If so, when and where?

Untroubling

John 14:1–7

"Do not let your hearts be troubled."

One after another the disciples questioned him. Their doubt, their fear, and at times, their numbskullery was painfully exposed at the Last Supper. The beloved disciple had already asked who on earth would betray the Master. Peter, at the edge of Jesus' arrest and the road to crucifixion, dumbly asked where Jesus was going. Thomas inquired how the disciples could know the way—apparently to nowhere, as he made it sound. Philip was about to ask to be shown the Father, displaying the fact that he had missed the point of just about everything. The beloved disciple kept on listening, at times perhaps shaking his head.

John realized that Jesus was sending a message that traveled beyond the immediate and intimate circle known as the Twelve. There was room at table for everyone, he seemed to want them to know. There was dwelling beyond the present upper gathering space. There was not only acceptance but welcome. There was a future to hope through to. All one had to do was lean on Jesus' shoulder, then buck up and follow.

Jesus knew, and John in his mature reflections understood, that within each of us is a homeless person. Our awareness of this self may be merely momentary, or it may be chronic. It may be doubt that comes and goes, or it may be a loneliness and sense of love-lessness that verges on cosmic despair. It may be a shrugging awareness of our imperfections and inconsistencies, or it may be a weight of guilt and shame that overwhelms us.

Jesus invited his faltering and faint-hearted followers to understand that they did not need inner resources or personal strength. He did not preach a gospel of self-reliance and rugged individualism. He did not even enjoin on them a binding set of regulations or insist on a way of perfection in the sort of detail we have fashioned since. He simply asked their faith in his person, their hope in his promise, their confident charity. He invited them to love in a way that would never patronize the infirm or belittle the backsliding but would, rather, offer to all an understanding heart.

As Jesus entered into his own love of a meal, a ritual, and the company of friends, as he entered into an encounter with sweat and dread and agony and fear of death, he invited them to something and somewhere better. He summoned them to God's house and its many mansions "so that where I am, there you may be also" (14:3). Jesus invited them to dream of home and to know that they were homeward bound. He primed them to recall that he would open the door, set the table, and lavish love upon them when they arrived at their destination.

The best gift Jesus gave and gives his fretful followers is this word that he wants them forever where he is—and that he will take them as they are, on their own wavering terms, even as they take tentative steps across the threshold.

God, take me into your arms and welcome me to the house of your heart. I have nowhere else to go, and I need you to be my home.

For Reflection

Christians believe that Christ in his suffering and dying carried the weight of all our misery, sin, and failing—the weight of everything that bears us down. When I think of the passion of Christ, how do I find myself carried and comforted, despite the images and remembrance of pain?

Greater Works

John 14:8–14

"Very truly, I tell you, the one who believes in me will also do the works that I do and, in fact, will do greater works than these."

A bird perches on a rough wooden rail, a full yellow cherry locked like a hard marble into its beak. It holds the fruit of a quest. It holds nourishment. It clasps sustenance to last for hours. All it has to do is bite down, fragment the fruit ball, eject a pit, and eat.

During a long discourse, Jesus told Philip that he and his company already had enough to last them a lifetime. He reminded them that they had received gifts as they had been initiated into mysteries. He startled them with a confidence that they would go, act, and, in some sense, outdo him, their teacher and Lord. Their influence would stretch over eons. We who have the benefit of retrospect see.

But at this point in the story, they were still perched and carrying the yellow cherry in their beaks. He reminded them that they had to bear down, break what they'd received into bits, and eat.

Living Lord, bearer of good fruit, steer me to the orchards of your truth. Remind me when to carry off fruit and when finally to eat. Let me know that you have given me all the nutriment I need.

For Reflection

What is the fruit I carry? Am I overdue to break it into smaller bits and eat?

Spirit-Power

John 14:15–31

"The Advocate, the Holy Spirit, whom the Father will send in my name, will teach you everything, and remind you of all that I have said to you."

Jesus lived in a world which primordially (and even somewhat primitively) believed, notes Marcus Borg (author of *Jesus: A New Vision*), in a spirit-world, a non-material world, which could and did interact with our everydayness. Lawgivers like Moses were led into deserts by the Spirit. Kings like David and Solomon were spirited leaders who raised armies, governed, accumulated wealth, and spun psalms and proverbs while enamored of Wisdom, that personal, godly Spirit who breathed life and crafted the world. Prophets like Elijah and Isaiah were fired by the Spirit and led others to new levels of awareness of goodness, holiness, and hope. Borg reminds us that Jesus was seen as having his inaugural when "the heavens opened" and there appeared "the Spirit descending upon him like a dove" (Borg, quoting Mark 1:10). The "primordial tradition" of Jesus' times expected, occasionally, just such incursions of the Spirit. The belief that there could be, and by nature must be, such intersections between the world of matter and the world of Spirit enabled belief that Jesus could be uniquely "a Spirit-filled person through whom the power of the Spirit flowed" (Borg, pp. 50–51).

John presumed as much. What he elaborated, though, is that Jesus, charismatic and heavenly himself, imparted that same Spirit-power to his followers, to those who would bear his mission and advance the realization of God's kingdom in the world. He also pressed the possibility that the very world that God's Spirit has hovered over, fired, nudged, inspired, touched with love, and pressed heavenward would also resist incursions, block intersections, ignore and deny, thus making matter, Mammon, the empirically measurable, its own deity.

John heard Jesus' anticipation that some would find the Holy Spirit too much for them.

Well, then, his message said, these timorous followers would have to have means to go on anyway. Keeping Jesus' words, loving, believing would have to be a way of rising. When the horizontal is barricaded, when journeyers lose heart, there is nowhere to go, after all, but up. The Spirit in the world would have to provide adequately fueled booster rockets. So be it.

Jesus, your own words imply that your Holy Spirit is insider and outsider at the same time. To the extent that your Spirit is outside me, let your fullness fall and fill my hollowings. Where your Spirit is already resident deep within, simply wake me up. Then, with you, I'll rise and go.

For Reflection

The origin and bounty of creation and the transformation wrought by Christ's incarnation assure that God loves the world and holds it in esteem, pronouncing it, to this day, "good." Why, then, this language of conflict between Christ and world, Spirit of truth and life here? Where have I seen and experienced meeting points between this world and the invisible one?

Vine-Clinging

John 15:1–11

"As the Father has loved me,
so I have loved you; abide in my love."

"Earth's the right place for love. I don't know where it's likely to go better," muses Robert Frost in his poem "Birches." He watches their weight and wave, their bending in the breeze, and expresses the wish to be "a swinger of birches," steady and supple in living and feeling.

We know—and it is gospel—that Earth both is and isn't the right place for love. It's the right place when we're branches on a sturdy vine. It's the right place when the suspicion and then the certainty breaks upon us that we are, finally, giving and receiving a love that is unconditional. It's the wrong place, though, if we expect love to be untroubled. It's the wrong place if we demand no separateness and no death. It's the wrong place if we can't tolerate the vagaries and self-doubt of our humanity. It's the right place, the Good News says, if we can love beyond our present seeing and believe that we are beloved. It's the wrong place if we presume that love ought to march to our drumbeat and play the tune of our will.

Jesus wanted, wants, for those who follow and for those who are friend to abide in love and to be filled with joy. He wanted and wants all this, knowing full well that we have limited resources, frailties and backslidings, self-deceptions, a readiness to embrace half-truths, vacillations in our devotion, and radical incapacity.

Immediately before the passage about the vine and the branches, Jesus was faced with questions from the beloved disciple, Peter, Thomas, and Philip: Who will betray you? Where are you headed? Will we need a map to get there? How about showing us all the who, what, when, where of God straight up? They continued to mumble among themselves, intending that he be within earshot: And now what's this "little while"? How about some plain-speaking?

In response, Jesus delivered challenge, assurance, the commitment of his person to these all-time experts at befuddlement.

They were who we are. With all the advantages of face-to-face contact, of seeing and hearing with their own eyes and ears, with question-and-answer dialogue, with the experience of miracles and interpretations, the apostles, the disciples, the beloved disciple continued to foray between shadow and cloud-break, sunshine and fog. As do we, even with the advantage of more than 2,000 years of faith. Even with the advantage of the guaranteed Word of God, sacramental life in a sacramental universe, and the testimony of saints telling us over and over how life is transformed and how all of everywhere is supercharged with grace.

Who will betray you? Where do we go? Why doesn't God show us something? Beyond all reason, we are at times the traitors, the lost, the sightless. Yet unless we're utterly fruitless, we're on the vine. And it is hard not to bear fruit when the one who loves us is so determined to keep us holding on.

"Earth's the right place for love," he might have said, as he kept bending down and keeps bending down still, to water, weed, fertilize, prune, and tie all of us to the arbor.

Vinegrower and vine, so sensitize me that I feel your loving touch as you tend me. Keep me clinging close to you and to all who branch from you truly, my brothers and sisters in whom your love abides.

For Reflection

Jesus is the patient gardener and the tireless teacher. What needs weeding in me? What demands repetition and reinstruction?

Friends

John 15:12–25

"I have chosen you out of the world."

Love is an invitation into polarities and paradox. Thomas Moore, in his wildly popular *Care of the Soul,* speaks of the hills and valleys, rises and falls, of love and being in love: "The high expectations and the rock-bottom experiences," the expectation that love will "be healing and whole" and the shock of the "hollow gaps" it can leave (Moore, p. 76). He also speaks of both the Creation story in Genesis and the Passion of Jesus as love stories (p. 82).

When Jesus dubbed his apostles and disciples "friends," he intended every implication of soul-mate in his use of that word. They were no sideline companions, no merely casual friends. He invested them with vital importance—branches on the vine, chips off the old block—and made it clear that they were to travel a love journey, a romantic adventure, with him.

Where?

From unexpected and privileged love to a world of resentment and misunderstanding. From the portals of divinity to the hell-gates of all too human jealousy and wrath.

Jesus invited those who loved him to a gala, a soulful festival of love. To get there, though, they had to traverse a minefield.

What's more, he instructed them to step on the mines.

For the sake of love's explosion. On the chance that mines blow up into arbors overflowing with grapevines.

Way to go, high and low.
Oh, God above, oh, drop-dead love.

For Reflection

Love makes us glad. Love drives us mad. Love turns us sad. How do I account for the vagaries of love? What does a constant God have to do with love's ups and downs?

What are the hollow spots of Christianity? What in Christian faith heals and makes whole?

Being True

John 15:26–27

"When the Advocate comes, whom I will send to you from the Father, the Spirit of truth who comes from the Father, he will testify on my behalf."

There are places where dolphins arch and curve—in a sine wave pattern of luxuriance and ease. No matter that they are feeding, exercising, doing what nature and God's providence have designed for them. They are artfully being themselves. A black hump appears and rolls over like musical phrase marks, and then another and another. They break water. And then they rise again.

Down the sandy shore, pelicans veer and edge in slow, erratic circles. At some point they will dive bomb, swift and defiant of the free-fall speed of gravity, and catch their latest snack. They, too, are working out the patterns of their lives and doing what they were made for.

Jesus, as confusing as he could sometimes be, was being true to his natures, human and divine. He was true teacher, savior, healer, prophet, and friend. The Spirit testified and testifies to who he was and is. That same Spirit testifies to our deep-down selves as well.

Who can tell in full what underlies our clockwork? Yes, we know, there is a time to be born and a time to die, a time to laugh and a time to weep, as Koheleth surmised so long ago. There is, truly, a time to love and a time to work, a time to press hard and a time to ease, a time to do and a time to pause.

What Jesus said, and the beloved knew, was that the Holy Spirit would jam our signals, scramble our genetic codes, start a rhythm in our heads that would reach the tips of our toes, and cause us, sometimes, to change course. We would be and become more and other than what we thought we were. We would turn into more. Yet that, too, would be part of the plan. We would arch, veer, slow, and speed, but it would be more than the fractals of nature that would drive us, make us jump, break our stride. It would be some other level of supernature that we could not begin to grasp.

We would only know it when it came, waving us like an ocean. It would command us to be what we were designed and destined for. To be that and also more.

Lord God, even in Christian ministry we are driven by deadlines, bottom lines, strategic plans, and end-of-the-road dates. We manage crises and put out fires. Remind us of what love can make, how the Spirit can bend us or turn us upside down.

For Reflection

When have I arched and played and swum free like a dolphin? Where was God in the story?

What might I need to discover, to do, and to be in order to be more truly the deep-down self of God's remarkable destiny for me?

O Discomforter

John 16:1–11

"Indeed, an hour is coming when those who kill you will think that by doing so they are offering worship to God."

By the time the Gospel according to John was written, believers had been driven out of the synagogues and endured persecution. The Christian Jews had become Jewish Christians, and there were Gentiles who had found a home among them. Women prophesied and prayed with the men, side by side. The Spirit was alive in them, and the Spirit-Advocate was guiding them in truth, even though the Spirit's truth rendered them unpopular, unwelcome, and, in many ways, worthy not only of disdain but of death. All this was true, even though the Spirit sometimes seemed to dazzle them with success.

So says the late Sulpician scholar, Raymond Brown. The beloved disciple, if not the apostle John, was, believes Brown, a "Spirit-guided leader" of a significant Christian community. What this community expected of the Spirit was conviction and hard knocks. Exterior charisms, as far as they were concerned, were flash-points but not true attractions. The masses wouldn't be won by razzle-dazzle, they resolved.

They may have been quite a grim crowd. For what they remembered of Jesus was not just the promises of abundant life and eternity but the promise that they'd be proven dead wrong about so much as well. If not they, then the world would. They'd ride out the storm if they could learn to slip quietly into a slim skiff, then stand still in it.

Among those who wanted healings, loaf-multiplications, wine made water, and calmed storms, Jesus' brand of discipline, love, and living water came sometimes as stuff too strong: head wind, storm surge, some unnamable roil. What could they count on?

They had hoped for a Spirit who would be Elijah's gentle breeze. All they had wanted was a bit of breather in their truth, a measure of the lackadaisical in their love.

This Jesus seemed, even at decades of distance, still to be demanding of them. They read it back to one another again and sighed the sigh of the resigned.

Holy Spirit, let me take you and embrace you when you are less Comforter than Discomforter, less Advocate on my behalf than Advocate for what I don't want, where I dread to go, and every why that stops my heart.

For Reflection

Dietrich Bonhoeffer popularized the phrase (and title) "the cost of discipleship." Spiritual writers since have treated the theme of costly grace with a nod to Bonhoeffer's understanding. As we consider Jesus' appeal face-to-face, what do we find costly in his call to come follow? As we consider his invitation over and over in a Spirit-filled church, what price do we pay for our yes?

What You Can Bear

John 16:12–22

"When a woman is in labor, she has pain, because her hour has come. But when her child is born, she no longer remembers the anguish because of the joy of having brought a human being into the world."

Perhaps the beloved disciple whispered from afar in Sister Madeleva's ear. Academic and sister, poet and college president, champion of women's theological empowerment and counselor to Dr. Tom Dooley, she had time to make of her life a prayer and love song. Throughout her life she won awards. She advised and cheered on not only the women of St. Mary's College but the renowned medical missionary to Laos, Tom Dooley, a Notre Dame man. From the 1940s on, she became known for encouraging Catholic Action at its best. In the late 1950s, she challenged and entertained readers with her spirited autobiography, *My First Seventy Years*.

Underneath a personality that won friends and drew admirers, and a productivity that propelled initiative upon initiative, she had a pensive, tender heart. Her reputation was for excellence, but her motivation was driven by love and, she admitted, some tears.

Madeleva took to heart the call of every Christian, every disciple, to be in some sense spiritual mother, bearer of Christ to the world. She was one who knew gestation, the long, mysterious coming-to-be of great ideas, good causes, and lasting friendship. Her poems tell us that. She was one who knew that the Spirit bore truth unbearable and bearable, and that lovers of Jesus would be pregnant with them. She knew that little whiles could be of short duration or long, since God's perspective on "little" may be millennial to us. Madeleva knew, too, the tender love of a mother who could pick up, dust off, and softly kiss a wounded child.

Sister Madeleva, woman of letters and leadership, knew the genuineness of the lines of our Lord's last discourse, and particularly one of them: "No one will take your joy from you" (16:22). But she also knew how love, especially in its divine form, could seem to cut holes in one's heart.

She had days in Oxford and Cairo, moments along the S-curves of St. Joseph's River in Indiana, and inside the Suez Canal. She also, in old age, had a first communion of sorts—the first time she received in a hospital. When she looked at Our Lady, as a mother standing beneath the cross, she knew something of glory and pain and little whiles that ache into eternity. She wrote:

Today the earth and sky are mute with woe
And every lip is dumb.
Holding You to my heart again I know
Peace and its price have come.
(From "The Thirteenth Station," in *The Four Last Things*, p. 156)

The beloved disciple must have whispered the story in her ear. He had first heard it on Holy Thursday and then lived it on Good Friday. He knew what strength of faith could bear, even when it seemed unbearable, even when a birth seemed unimaginable.

Tell me, Lord, what can I not bear yet? What do you want me to bear to the world? And how will I know the while that I carry?

For Reflection

As I recall the Stations of the Cross, in which one do I find myself most present? Where am I amid the bystanders?

Manner of Speaking

John 16:23–33

"The hour is coming when I will no longer speak to you in figures, but will tell you plainly of the Father."

Sometimes we believe that if we make some changes we'll finally get it right. Quit a job and take a new one, move, rest more and work less. Get out of that relationship, strike up a new one, scheme about how to live our dream. Make a retreat and turn all our regrets into bright flashes of holiness. Get better, no matter what it takes.

Sometimes, though, we realize that altering externals, shifting our circumstances and situations, investing ourselves in something or someone new still won't satisfy a longing or fill a hole.

There's something we're wanting to say, even though we know neither what nor how. There's something we're pining for, even though we barely guess what.

Madeline De Frees, known for thirty-some years as poet and creative writing coach Sister Mary Gilbert, continued to rely on imagery in order to write, even though the entire landscape of her life was, of late, transformed. If she wanted to speak of love, death, work, God, or a flash of human fear, she had to speak (in *Magpie on the Gallows*) of monks in choir, roadkill, splitting two-by-fours, Galileo's daughter on a sea voyage, and bright lynx eyes. Changing her whole life around didn't negate her need for figure, metaphor, or even circuitous language. We want pictures as well as words.

Jesus and the apostles, near the end, egged each other on.

He'd say: "A joy day is coming. Ask for it!"

They'd say: "Say what?"

He'd say: "I'll put it to you straight. Soon I'll be gone. And then some."

They'd say: "We hear you now. God sent you, yes?"

He'd say: "And you'll scatter off to hide in your homes."

They'd say: "And?"

He'd say: "Peace and courage! You'll hang on."

They'd say: "And?"

He'd say: "It's won."

Poetry needs a color to the earthen hut, descriptions to satisfy eleven quizzical minds, elaboration of the jewels on heaven's gate, some mention of the pitch and timbre of the voice of God. And hyperbolic exclamations of what everything else might be like.

Sister Mary Gilbert or Madeline, whatever her phase, still needed her word pictures.

"Say what?" the disciples and lovers asked for us.

Perhaps that was why Thomas Merton, after his swoops into political writing, hermitage days, calligraphy, and Zen fell into a nurse's arms and then opened his mouth long enough to say how much dead silence meant.

Jesus tried to tell them.

At times, there is nothing to say but ever after.

Tell me, Lord, how to ask for silence, how to pray the happy end, how to hearten myself for the courage you say to take. I swallow hard. You say: "Be still." I hear: "Shut up."

For Reflection

Why, in the end, do we picture so little as it is? And why do we say so much?

At-One-Ness

John 17:1–19

"Holy Father, protect them in your name that you have given me, so that they may be one as we are one."

Though the world was adversarial, the followers of Jesus were sent into it. There was still work to be worked, and God's name was still, by far, by wide, so little known. Jesus remained, to most, a small-town preacher, a little-nation wonder, a mystery of life and birth, with his pre-existence, his foreknowledge, his redeeming work, his divinity next to unguessed.

So, on the eve of his departure, he asked protection for them, the hangers on who had actually, so far, hung on. They would need it—a spiritual sort of bullet-proof vest, a religious kind of body armor. They would need the stamina that survives sleeplessness, drought, penury, marginalization, and total shunning. They would need, at times, internal camouflage; at other times they would need an aurora borealis of personality that could arise from within. There were times, after all, when visibility would threaten their lives. At other moments, though, invisibility could imperil their mission.

Jesus knew. And so he prayed for them, praised them, encouraged them, and entrusted them with mission.

Eternal life was the perspective he left them.

The love of the Trinity—indeed, the very relationship that was the nature of God—would be their refuge and drive. Even though they did not yet know of Three-in-One or even what would happen on a third day.

They just knew, with him, that they were going on. In arms.

At heart, Lord, all of us want at-one-ness—with love, with the peace that passes understanding, with the All-in-All. Make me one with you, the Only, the Every, the One with Creator and Sanctifying Spirit. We live, I know, in a beautiful and a dangerous world. Let me be at one with the good, so that I may discern clearly. And so lead me to distinguish clearly opportunity from danger, and occasion to move out from time to seek cover.

For Reflection

There is an at-one-ness of heart that we can experience with our inner being, with the outer world, with strangers and friends, with a special love, with the cosmos, and with God. What type of at-one-ness do I most intensely feel? When? For what at-one-ness ought I pray?

An at-one-ness with other Christians has long been a hope and goal. Pope John Paul II, writing before the dawn of the new millennium, prayed for a "dialogue of love" so that the whole world might hear unconfusedly Christ's saving word (*Ut Unum Sint*, #47). How have I contributed to efforts to increase understanding among Christians?

Glory's Shine

John 17:20–26

"The glory you have given me I have given them."

What is flabbergasting about our Lord is the confidence he has in our feeble flesh and wandering minds. God, we know from the wisdom of the ages, has glory, comes in glory, shines forth glory. Glory, as the ancient languages have it (*shekinah* in Hebrew, *doxa* in Greek) is the weight of splendor God bears. D. Moody Smith, Scripture scholar, says of glory that it is, at its simplest (and then again at its most incredibly complex, from our standpoint) "the quality of God as God" (Smith, p. 121). Glory is "God's reality, his real presence, as it is manifest to humankind" (p. 122). Thus, all glory is as much as we can bear and also too much.

God's glory is light at its brightest, beauty at its loveliest, music at its most thrillingly harmonious, goodness at its noblest, and love at its most totally enfolding. Glory is the quality of God in Christ, and God's glory shone forth to Jesus' followers in moments of miracles—healings, transfiguration on the mountain—and in moments of abject humility—his understatements, his silences, footwashing, lavish forgiveness and compassion, surrender to the cross.

What Jesus said to his followers, in that long night of the last discourse, was that the glory of God evident in him was theirs, too. He saw gift and promise in them. He heard the gospel in the beat of their hearts. Who knows why? Surely not they. But glory was theirs and, since the Son's implications have proven to be timeless, glory is ours, too.

"Shine, Jesus, Shine" sing the schoolchildren. As they sing, they shine. "Gloria in excelsis Deo" intones the choir, skilled in its four-part harmonies, and they turn glorious.

So it goes. God's godliness, God's reality, God's pressing presence pours through our fragmented selves and pools out around us. There is no way to fathom why God would give so much of God's self away. There is no way to reason why it would be ours to share and display. There is no sense to God's glory falling upon us, penetrating us, and coming to stay.

The only sense is that the beloved disciple's beloved said so. And a word of glory is, if nothing else, trustworthy.

Why me, Lord? I bear no beauty, no majesty, small truth, less love. So why would you choose to manifest yourself in my frail and passing person? Be glory, as heavy as I need.

For Reflection

Jesus associates the making-known of God and the manifestation of love with God's glory. How have I experienced glory in my life, and how have I grown in my understanding of God from that experience?

Nightwatch

John 18:1–27

Simon Peter and another disciple followed Jesus.

Marcus Borg reminds us, in *Jesus: A New Vision,* that everything John's gospel tells of Jesus is filtered through the gathered-in experience of a growing and well-established community. Coming from as late in the first century of the Common Era as it does, it portrays Jesus as clear about his mission, aware not only of his destiny but his pervasive divinity. Jesus is conqueror, Pantocrater, master of all situations and especially of himself.

He doesn't always look that way in the other gospels, which show moments of ambivalence and hesitation. John's gospel omits the sweat, the bartering with the Father, and the dismay at the sleepiness of the men he needed in Gethsemane. John's gospel simply states that Jesus went into a garden. There he was beset by soldiers and police, to whom he uncoweringly identified himself. Amid the chaos, Jesus censured Peter for swordplay, restored a slave's mutilated and detached ear, and went forth, bound, to drink the cup. He proclaimed before Annas that he had preached openly; and he asked for an indication of what the powers-that-be felt was so wrong about what he had stood for. Peter, meanwhile, was about the business of denying his connections with Jesus. Jesus somehow retained his assurance, giving no hint of uncertainty, no indicators that he was suffering blows to his ego—no, or next to no—murmurs of human puzzlement or regret. He continued self-possessed. And so it began. And so it went.

But, in the midst of this more majestic account of the beginning of the passion, we might read with the sensitivity of a lover. We might ask if Jesus flinched even a little bit when he later told Pilate that, if he (Jesus) were a worldly king, he would have followers fighting for him (18:36). Did he begin to wonder, even as Peter was first questioned in the high priest's courtyard, where they all had gone? Did he not cringe to think of Peter warming himself and answering lamely? By John's understanding of Jesus, he would have known.

Did Jesus for a moment wonder if his humanity had somehow misspoken, when he began the cycle of questioning and was about to be passed on to Caiaphas and then to Pilate? Was he prepared to speak of truth and wonder if anyone at all had understood? Did he, for a fleeting moment, entertain the thought that the truth on which he had staked his life might suffer mishap and be lost on all? His disciples were free to a man—and to a woman—to deny him, change their minds, and forget the whole thing once he had seen the next hours through.

Did Jesus look off, before the flogging and crowning were underway, in hopes that he might catch a glimpse of one of them and find some comfort in that face? Would he have been relieved to know that one light-robed young man, a beloved and sensitive soul, had waited from night into break of day, trudging from station to station in the shadows.

God knows. Did the God-in-him at that moment also know?

Jesus, Lord, as you mounted the ladder to heaven and simultaneously began the slow slide toward suffocation and blood, did you shed enough of your Godhood to want some human comfort? Did you want, as I do, to know that someone listens to my heart, watches my face while hearing my words, and wants to stay? Were you hoping, in some small way, that someone who loved you would see the whole thing through?

For Reflection

When have I stayed by in someone's suffering? When have I watched with God all night? Ever? Almost?

Great Horned Night

John 18:28–40

So Pilate went out to them and said,
"What accusation do you bring against this man?"

There are nights the owls hollow out. Those nights, dark becomes garden, torch becomes doom, sweat becomes prayer, friends become sleep.

Mary Oliver speaks of screech owls, saw-whets, snowy owls, the friendlier, more companionable sort. But of the great horned, she says: "They are the pure wild hunters of our world. They are swift and merciless upon the backs of rabbits, mice, moles, snakes, even cats sitting in dusky yards, thinking peaceful thoughts" ("Owls," in *Owls and Other Fantasies*, p. 15).

The night of foot-washing, table-setting, morsel-dipping, and long speech was a great horned night. It was a night for a hustle of soldiers and police, for a scattering of followers, for a confusion in courts and tribunals.

It was a night for truth to be left an open question and royalty a dislodged crown.

It was a night and then a morning when all the world would seem to want Barabbas.

Lord, there are times I cannot want you. Yet I do not desire the triumph of evil. I do not want guilt and bloodbath. Make me a gentler sort, a snowy owl.

For Reflection

In all the creature world, there is death and predation as well as hooting and nights that lull. We humans, though, are expected to use intelligence and freedom for the sake of truth and justice. We are made by God capable of choosing the better part, the better way, in all things. Why do we opt for less, for a lie, for the strangle-hold of fear? Why do we even, at times, prefer evildoing?

"Crucify Him!"

John 19:1–16

"Away with him! Away with him! Crucify him!"

Dr. Michael Willett Newheart has noted that African-American writing since the War between the States has linked the lynchings of black men with the crucifixion of Jesus. He tells, too, of a time when he was fired as a missionary for his unconventional methodology. His "trial" took place before two church mission boards. A biblical scholar and a teacher with an innovative and admittedly experimental style, he tells his own life and the Gospel of John in down-home, street-smart, backyard-wise poetry, puns, and stream-of-consciousness prose. After Dr. Newheart was let go, he made a retreat. No more Costa Rican mission. He went to a Catholic center, visited with a spiritual director, and made the Stations of the Cross. "I connected Jesus' Via Dolorosa with my own," he offers, writing in *Word and Soul: A Psychological, Literary, and Cultural Reading of the Fourth Gospel.*

Each one of us has our passion. Whatever and whenever it takes place, it both is and is not like the passion of the Christ.

Some injustice is done to us. Some unwarranted evil and pain befalls us. What is needful, though, if we are beloved, is that our passion and crucifixion serve some good. Christ's passion became, and John's standing by turned into, our along-sidedness in trial and the triumph of mercy. The "upward" pole of the cross must, Newheart says, translate into, "Up, word!" and "UpWord." Why?

Because even though Christ is risen, "Crucifixions continue" (p. 122). Who can say what untruth and fright and power play and stiff-neckedness can do?

Though they can't ever be ultimately victorious. The aftermath of that bad Good Friday proves it so.

Lord, I gaze upon your crucified figure from the distance of centuries of devotion and art. I watch a film by Mel Gibson depicting your last hours. Yet the pain I most fix on is my own. Release me from myself so I may stand others' pain with them, and thus stand also in your own pain for us, for me.

For Reflection

How, indeed, do I relate the passion of Christ, and particularly the people's demand for his crucifixion, to life around me and my own life? Do I even begin to let myself feel it? Where am I in the crowd?

Being Truth

John 19:17–25a

Pilate answered, "What I have written I have written."

The editors of Catholic Exchange published, in mid-2004, *A Guide to the Passion: 100 Questions about "The Passion of the Christ"*. Among so many, many topics of discussion about Mel Gibson's renowned film is the topic of the inscription which Pilate ordered to be hammered onto the cross. The editors of the guidebook note that the film does not include a segment reported by John: the objections to the sign. So this counter-comment by Pilate is missing, too. We are left to interpret the missing section—and to speculate that the film's sympathetic portrait of Pilate's wife and, to some extent, of Pilate is meant to portray the possibility of nascent faith.

Yet it seems an important commentary on how a ruler can be manipulated by a stirred up crowd, when they tap into his own fear of reprisals from higher authorities. There's an inner anger in Pilate which may or may not hint that he cares a whit about Jesus. The drama of the sign seems to be a bit of flexing of his authoritative muscle and an expression of a measure of spitefulness for his having been backed into a corner on this crucifixion. The real issue, however, is Jesus' true identity. In truth, Pilate barely began to inquire into that identity. It too profoundly intimidated him. And so he resorted to a sign which may have been a purposeful insult to the accusers or a mockery of their religious in-fighting. A king! Of course.

For the beloved disciple, however, the disciple in love, Jesus was certainly always princely at the very least. In the end, and really throughout the Book of Glory in this gospel, he was seen as kingly, too. He led by example and encouragement, he saw and interpreted the larger picture, he pursued his vision and his destiny, and he was willing to pay whatever price was needed for his people. The sign, despite any ambivalence or put-down of the accusers on the part of Pilate, read rightly. As far as John and his future community were concerned, the act of crucifixion and its association with criminality were the lies. The inscription, however intended, revealed the irrepressible truth.

Jesus' identity would out. He was, while God and King, also the most authentic human being. There was no pretense in him, no intentional obfuscation of his meaning, no shadow side which he needed to take pains to conceal.

Jesus of Nazareth, Jesus the Christ, was as real as one could be in his passion—his passion for life and for love, that is, and not only the passion he suffered in a night and a day of torment and torture.

Being real is imaged for us in two other symbol-laden statements of this passage, aside from the sign which proclaims, in other words: "Here's who he is: Your leader. Your Davidic ruler. Your awaited one." The other two statements or moments are these: 1) John's insistence that Jesus carried his own cross alone and 2) his comment on the seamless garment, which the soldiers decided to leave intact.

Being authentic, being true, being real is like that. One ultimately has to shoulder one's cross and take on whatever weight must be borne. One has, that is, responsibilities and a price to pay just for being who and what one is called to be. And one has to have about oneself something that is integral and whole. One has to learn how to wear life well and how to be well-woven and intact in public.

Jesus' identity was simply who he was: man of Nazareth, rabbi, gentle healer, emergent King, Lord of history. His true self had to be, in the end, solitary, just weighty enough, and of a piece.

Perhaps someone noticed. Perhaps Pilate was just a Gentile coward with a little authority. But for one solid moment he had asked about truth. In the midst of this questioning, Jesus proved whole unto himself, filled with integrity, and true to his truth. Pilate, after the fateful interview, managed to post a sign, which is to say that he managed, intentionally or unintentionally, to do one true thing.

King of all nations and Lord of every story, let me always recall that you are king of hearts—mine, ours, even of those who notice you grudgingly.

For Reflection

Christ the King is a resplendent feast, marking the last Sunday of the liturgical year in gold and glory. But Good Friday also celebrates Christ's kingship. So what do these two observances say about the Christian understanding of kingship, of divine monarchy?

When am I most real, most authentic, most sure of my identity? And when not? What does love have to do with it, and truth, and God's own integrity?

Stabat Mater

John 19:25b–27

Then he said to the disciple, "Here is your mother."

There is a prayer posted in a side chapel at the National Shrine of the Immaculate Conception in Washington, DC. It begins, "Mary, our Mother of Africa, hear the drumbeat of our prayers."

There are black Madonnas, brown ones, yellow ones, red ones, white. Our Lady of Czestochowa, of Guadalupe, of the Philippines, of the Navajo people, of Fatima. She appears and vanishes, reappears and consoles, fades and then comes back, century after century.

Mary, Mother of Jesus, has been herald and hero, comforter and countess, remotely regal in her jeweled gowns and crowns, and also pictured sewing, cooking, and hanging clothes on a line. She, who never traveled much of Africa except for a sojourn Egypt, became the African Queen, thousands of years after her son worried aloud about who would look after her. She became patroness of the Americas, two continents, north and south, though they remained unknown in her day. She was made matriarch of the world and goes on.

Sister Elizabeth Ruth Obbard, a British Carmelite, has written, in *Ruth and Naomi: A Story of Friendship, Growth, and Change,* of her motherless childhood, her curiosity about her welcoming, quaintly different, and not quite decipherable grandmother. As a young woman, she was drawn to an artist's depiction of the friendship of Ruth and Naomi, an affectionate, maternal-filial friendship. It represented a longing within her.

Later, after adult years as a nun living among women who could be warm or cool, expansive or remote, in-gathering or off-putting, even in their silence, she realized that there came a point at which she left Ruth behind and had, in a sense, become Naomi.

Jesus, in giving his mother to the beloved John, knew that there was something of the biblical Ruth and something of Sister Elizabeth Ruth in his followers and his beloved, then and now. There was in them, and is in us, something that wants security, acceptance, protection, shelter, warmth, and unconditional love. There was in them, and is in us, soothing that needs the ideal mother. He gave her, Mary, so that the disciples and we would find one day that we all, male and female, could be mother, too.

For every disciple, every lover of Jesus must, in the end, find his or her way to bear Christ to the world. Someone somewhere needs the mother of Bethlehem, the mother from Nazareth, the mother in Jerusalem, the mother at the cross to appear in us.

Mary, mother me, and assist me as I become, by your Son's love, mother of some one or two who need you from me.

For Reflection

When I think of Mary as mother, how do I picture her? How does she relate to the church at large? How to me? What holy mothering do I need?

In what way do I see myself called to spiritual motherhood in relation to another and others? How do I practice it?

Consummation

John 19:28–42

When Jesus had received the wine, he said, "It is finished."

For those of us who stroll the sands, there are days when the sight of a fishing boat stalled offshore for trawling and a bright-sailed catamaran catches us and fascinates. We glance about and notice a few boys on surf boards and children in turquoise and royal blue tubes flopped in water, head first and feet up. Overhead eleven or twelve water birds go zigzag and raggedy ann, all inept at v-formation. A long kite wobbles, its wielder nowhere in sight. A couple, far too old and rippled for their suits, waddle the beach while the same slim woman who comes to the pier every clear day casts her fishing rod again against the wind, her t-shirt flapping over faded shorts, her bare legs and feet browned in her sandals. She seems not to need to clutch her baseball cap as she twirls a cigarette not far from her uncurled silver bob. In the aftermath of a storm, a horseshoe crab has washed up. A split sand dollar, rouge and gray with waste, protrudes just enough that the walkers can avoid cut feet.

When we are in love, when our lives and dreams have been reconstituted by love, we smile at all such things, dogs splashing frantically, beach umbrellas up and down, the stray teen surfer, escaped in the off season from school, plying his board despite all the wrong tide.

We chuckle to ourselves at the world's loveliness. Yet we know, all too soon, how suddenly the spell of love can break. We look out, beyond fishing boat, beyond catamaran, and think we've sighted a mast. It must be, must be, the small but so significant sloop we've awaited, bearing our long-lost love. Then we look again, and no mast stands at all—not a single one across the whole span where skyline meets the sea.

There was a day when those who had chortled at palm branches saw not the awaited mast but an unwanted barred pole on which a man hung. It stayed. No matter how they tried to look away. There he was, stripped of every possibility, every promise. Every second they'd invested in watching, waiting, praying seemed gone.

Whether a dog sprang up and licked their hands or an unknowing child did a stubborn little dance, they could respond no more than to shrink into the silent folds of their dusty robes, expressionless.

It could not be, they thought, that everything that glistened, foamed, cooled, relieved, and roused in them a sense of play and then an everlasting hope was gone.

But so it seemed. And they were left there, marooned, forlorn.

I have too often felt God-forsaken, too, my Lord. Give me memory of the joy days and confidence in the love. Don't let me dress myself in numbness when all the world breaks. Bring back, bring back. Remind me that you breathe wind into my sails and make each fair day break.

For Reflection

But what about the blood and water?

What about the myrrh and aloes?

In the Garden

John 20:1–10

Early on the first day of the week, while it was still dark, Mary Magdalene came to the tomb.

Even on the hottest day in August, when the heat index is 110 degrees, one can still find a place—somewhere—where a cooling wind will whip through one's hair and clothes. One has only to look for the right piers, the right boardwalks. A person might be looking for a prayer place, some solace. He or she may be sounding the deep for some word of wisdom or hoping it might plummet with the suddenness of a pelican dive, straight from above.

We are, at times, the Magdalene mourning, the Magdalene bereft, the lost and lovesick stunned almost to nothingness and unable to imagine what might be next.

Mary went to the tomb because there was nothing else to do. Sleep had no meaning, nor did waking up. Company filled no emptiness, nor did solitude offer respite. She came alone to where the one, the only one, who had seen through to the heart of her pain, her heart that longed for lasting love, had been laid to rest. She came alone to where they had left for dead the one who knew how her soul ached for the infinite majesty of God and genuine human touch. Then she saw that the stone had been moved.

Alone again, she could do nothing more than turn to the two who had, in their own way, loved Jesus. She rushed, quizzical, to the volatile Peter and to the one they called the beloved, John. At her word, they ran, the younger dashing ahead, the elder arriving a little later. The deferential youth let Peter look first. They saw wrappings, a folded cloth. Then they left, wondering what these abandoned linens could mean and why a gesture of neatness had so struck them, that strange folding of the cloth which had covered his ruined face.

Mary Magdalene, it appears, had followed after their running but then stayed behind at the empty tomb when they left.

Love sometimes springs into action, puzzles over the unanswerable, and then runs home, needful of familiarity in the face of upheaval. That is what Peter and the beloved disciple did. They went back to sort things out on what was, at least temporarily, home ground. At other times, love lingers. Love paces a street where two had spoken as they walked. Love loiters where, in a soft moment, eyes had met and lives had connected with such force that nothing could ever remain the same. Or love stalls and tries to catch its breath in a cemetery, in a quiet garden, in an unpeopled park as it tries to grasp the fact that something that had been is no more and that someone who had been the embodiment of energy, purpose, and holy passion was now the stranger, a cold corpse. Or simply was gone. How can a lover swallow that? How can one, with a whole world altered again, and this time sunk to an emptiness worse than any before; how can such a one imagine living on?

And so she lingered there, like the watcher at a hot south fishing pier, stunned, waiting for God knew what.

Teacher, lover and brother of the living and the dead, wait with me. Stir me with some hope when I wander aimlessly, beside myself. Give me something to go on.

For Reflection

A park, a beach front, or a palm desert may be places where beauty promises to break through a sullen sadness of our souls. Cemeteries and memorials can, too. Where do I go when I need to face my uncertainty and grief? What small things there bring comfort?

Dan Brown, in his super-achieving novel *The Da Vinci Code*, perpetuates a legend that won't die: the legend that Jesus and Mary

Magdalene were married lovers. Why does this legend continue to hold appeal? What do I make of the love which the church celebrates in Easter story and saint's day, when it comes to the traditional story of this Mary?

Wisdom Woman

John 20:11–18

Mary Magdalene went and announced to the disciples, "I have seen the Lord."

There are women, earthmother types, who possess an uncommon wisdom, gleaned not from formal learning but from observance of the most common things. They have watched how crabapples plump and how birds zero in, just at the end of season, on the softness of those apples' centers. They know what stray cats or even squirrels will crawl the porch for—a small bowl of milk or a pod of black walnuts, bagged in plastic from the front yard. They know how families fend and feud, and they invent occasions to gather them. They know when wool should be shorn and how it must be knit for winter warmth. They can read moods, incipient illnesses, and the in-breaking of fate just by noticing a change in someone's gait. A story circulates, a mysterious stranger arrives in town, a dog howls at night, and they know something beyond calculation or logical explanation.

Wisdom women midwife, nurse, feed, comfort, bury, breed, lift up, and simply listen. They can decode a word and decipher worlds of meaning where others sit stupefied and silent.

Mary Magdalene was one of those wisdom women. She had been burned and bedeviled by life, but because of that she had plumbed the depths. She was ready to recognize not only an uncommonly nice man but also a messiah when she saw one. And she did. She stood by, saying little, and she circled back to the starting point, a tomb, when confusion set in. She waited, knowing that amid clouds and flowers some sense would arise. Wisdom browses, she knew, by backroads, and it lays banquets which may start with deceptively simple fare, amid houses of stone and sky.

She was ready to hear a message for the ages in a single muttered word. And then she heard it: "Mary!"

It was the gardener—of Gethsemane, of Eden Regained. And so she went to tell the others.

Spirit of the simplest and Spirit of all, give me wisdom to wait, to listen, to take in, to know. And give me a voice to speak whatever is good, true, beautiful, and holy as you summon a world of surprise amid the ordinary to steer me.

For Reflection

Kathleen Norris has written of "Quotidian Mysteries," those everyday blessings and benefits and truths that mark our lifespan and speed our growth. What wisdom have I gained by returning to places of perplexity? What simple truths have come to me in solitude at times of great stress?

What do I imagine came next for Mary Magdalene, after she announced the resurrection to the apostles?

Through the Door, Shalom

John 20:19–23

Jesus came and stood among them and said, "Peace be with you."

It was T.S. Eliot, in his groundbreaking twentieth century poem, "The Waste Land," who quoted St. Paul and his expression of the longing of the human heart, Oriental and Occidental, for that "peace that passeth understanding."

After the collapse of everything and amid baffling, fear-dogged days, what the disciples wanted most was peace. The Hebrew concept of shalom is deeper than that peace that is wished in a perfunctory greeting at Mass, more lasting than an expression on a greeting card, more profound even than an intercessory prayer. Shalom is what one longs for, experiences in fleeting moments, and always hopes to keep. It is a thorough-going assurance that one is well physically, sound in mind, balanced emotionally, secure upon the land, at ease with family and companions, spending one's energy appropriately, flourishing in one's time and culture, fittingly awake and at rest, held in esteem and affection by those who matter, understood in weakness, forgiven in sin, appreciated for goodness, affirmed in triumph, and right with God.

The totality of shalom is, thus, hard to come by and harder to hold for long.

Yet it is what Jesus, after virtually complete abandonment, wished for his disciples and friends. Peace cannot be realized by utterly normal means. So Jesus bequeathed to them the Holy Spirit.

Shalom can be had and held only if one is overtaken, made whole by the divine, and given power to impart wholeness to others.

So they received the Spirit.

So, in time, they began to recognize the gift and rely upon it.

Soon.

Descend upon me, Spirit of peace. Assure me that I am triply blest by holy wholeness. Then let me go forth to be peace for others, too.

For Reflection

When do I say, from the bottom of the heart, St. Francis' peace prayer: "Lord, make me an instrument..."? Can I say it now?

In what sense is Jesus the fullness of peace for me? When am I most aware of it?

And Again, Peace

John 20:24–31

A week later his disciples were again in the house,
and Thomas was with them.

Especially in this age of frequent job changes and unprecedented mobility, we find ourselves being linked to others' work, family lives, leisure activities, circle of friends, and then abruptly having to leave everything that has become familiar and home. We pass and repass, touching close for a moment and then having to move on. Try as we might to keep contact, to call, to e-mail, to come back for a holiday visit or a summer vacation, we soon know that something has been let go. Alice Walker has reminded us of an oft-quoted African-American saying: You can't stand in the same river twice. We find that bonds were not forged as tightly as we might have thought, we come back and see all the scenery transformed, and we learn that life without us has gone on. Eventually we close the book on still another phase and remember the persons only by the echoes of their names, the notations in an address book, the phantoms that appear in dreams.

Thomas may have been about the business of closing a book. The apparent Christ had died. The motley crew of apostles was all disjointed. One had stayed by, one had outright lied and denied, one had hanged himself, and nine others, himself included, had scattered into the humid night, fleeing the flame of soldiers' torch lights and fearing scorch by association. Not very long ago, Thomas had asked the Master to show the way (14:5). Jesus, with a touch of incredulity, had replied that the Twin had clearly missed the point somewhere along the way. The rabbi had insisted to Thomas that he himself was it. The Twin had been scratching his head ever since. Was he to think that Jesus, this purported Messiah, was *halakah*, was the way of walking, was somehow more than the law? And what could it mean that he shortly went forth to walk the way of the cross?

So Thomas had shaken the dust from his feet, for a time at least. And then he came back, only to have all of them berate him and then regale him with tales of how a dead man had returned to them through locked doors. And then, with Thomas there, Jesus did it again. He came through, pronouncing peace upon them for the third time.

Thomas would go down in religious history with "Doubting" used as his nickname more than "Didymus," or "Twin." But only because he finally decided to return, to rejoin, to pray, to stay in one place, and to be open enough to exclaim, "My Lord and My God!" Thomas' doubt is remembered because he recovered the way and believed.

Tradition says he went to India and evangelized there. He evangelized elsewhere, too: everywhere that someone silently at Eucharist has breathed his prayer.

My Lord and my God! Wonder in me still. Relieve my doubts, unfear my fears, and free me from my unfreedoms.

For Reflection

Why do I believe without seeing? What have I seen that has helped my belief?

Gone Fishing

John 21:1–14

They went out and got into the boat,
but that night they caught nothing.

If we live near the ocean, there are days when we collect perfect shells to display in baskets and bowls, and days when we collect broken shells to crush into our driveway pavement or to strew around our plants or across the top of an end table in bits or around a lamp. There are days when we collect no shells at all.

When events have been too much, and we have no feeling left worth mentioning, no thought we're capable of interpreting, we turn to the rhythm of the mundane and routine. Simon Peter had to go fishing. It was something usual, something he could manage, something he knew. Others went with him. It hardly seemed to matter that they were coming back without a catch.

Then, once more, they were thrust into a world that countered expectation and brooked no explanation. A man on shore hailed them, advising them where to cast their nets. Suddenly they were hauling them in, nets overfull. As they approached shore, they had a fleeting flash of recognition of a figure, even though their eyes had not yet refocused. Their lives, as a matter of fact, had not yet refocused, slung as they had been from despair to hope, from heartbreaking confusion to confounded miracle, from scaredy-cat fear of arrest and grisly death to halting readiness for whatever might be asked of them next.

Like as not, they would have preferred to fish on, to hang "No Trespassing" warnings on the masts of their boats along with "Do Not Disturb" signs on their minds and souls.

But there he was again, unmistakable. One, the much loved, knew it first. Peter threw off his clothes and jumped in to swim. Some one or two rowed. The others just dragged the nets. What now?

Jesus bent and cooked breakfast on a charcoal fire he had started.

There are times, Lord, when I've had enough of you. There are times I'd prefer to be left alone because I've been through too much upheaval. But give me whatever spurt of energy it takes to welcome you again. Smile at me. Then give me a good breakfast.

For Reflection

Making a meal for someone can be humdrum. When, though, is it full of meaning and symbol? When is being served and fed something momentous?

Resume

John 21:15–19

"Do you love me?"

What might it mean to be a fisherman who is asked instead to go feed and tend sheep? What might it mean to be expected to watch the roll and rise of pasture lands and hills rather than of clouds and breakers and beach? What might it mean to have to measure, not the arch and splash of mighty fish in lake or sea, but the meaning of the yap and herding instinct of dogs at one's heels? And this, after having been asked, early and enigmatically, to go fishing for people?

We all know that Jesus spoke symbolic language, that the structure of his thoughts was often metaphoric. He talked often of sowers and seed, housewives and coins, darkness and light, and himself as water, bread, wine. Who could make it all out?

But what kept happening to Simon Peter was more than merely being urged to stretch his literal mind to the more figurative. He was being asked to stake his life on this questioner, this commander, this reappearer, this haunter whom he had followed with joy, with vacillation, and, yes, he confessed, with regret. He was being asked to lead, despite what he knew to be his incompetence and unreliability.

Whatever was next was the most supreme test of his love. There was no other way to say it.

It was not just a matter of a promise exacted at a beach. Not just a matter of a profession of faith dredged up from the morass of his surprise and fatigue.

No, this was an end to something.

The one who had cooked breakfast was cooking him. He was becoming some paschal offering. He would be smeared on doorposts and lintels, he feared, or hanged upside down on some desolate hill.

Meanwhile, yes, of course, he would feed whomever. Lambs. Sheep.

It wasn't just about changing landscape and livelihood. Of this much, of more to come and more than he'd ever wanted, he was sure.

Lord, you invite me beyond my imaginings and beyond my capacities. I need you to feed me and tend me as I go, black sheep, lost sheep that I am, to whatever next thing love asks.

For Reflection

When have I experienced a jarring change of occupation and/or people's, or the church's, expectations of me? What about it seemed to come from God? Was there anything about it which seemed not to be a matter of vocation and invitation to growth? How did I, do I, sort it out?

Living On

John 21:20–25

So the rumor spread in the community
that this disciple would not die.

The scientific discovery of evidence of the Big Bang and an expansion of the universe that goes on and on has raised unexpected questions about the resurrection. One phase of the story has to do with the fate of Jesus of Nazareth and how that affects prognostication about our continuation beyond death. Scripture speaks of us, too, being caught up with the Lord in the air (1 Thess 4:17), morphing into the mode of glorified body, and gathering with lamps trimmed, like virgins bent on getting into the wedding feast. Imagining the possibility of everlasting life is possible only to the person of faith. That's one thing.

The other thing, more challenged by Hubble-Hawking cosmos, is belief in the coming to be of new heavens, new earth—the transformation of all matter into something touched and diamond-struck by resurrection power. The likes of Ted Peters, Robert John Russell, Michael Welker, and John Polkinghorne have tossed around the impact of the anticipated scenarios of our long-term future on our notions of the end of the world. Reasonable science projects a melding of spacetime and an ultimate a) wide and infinite fizzle, or b) white hot "big crunch"—either of which will occur on some far off day when the world as we know it fritters off and impossibly away or falls into a hopelessly dense black hole. Either looks unlivable. The end time, which faith foresees as messianic reign, would appear, in science's scenarios, to arrive with nothing for a Messiah to do and no sensible future, no aftermath of judgment, into which bystander or disciple or any living, breathing, or simply planetary thing could continue.

Polkinghorne (as quoted in *Resurrection: Theological and Scientific Assessments*, ed. by Peters, Russell, and Welker) muses that perhaps we will pass on as information. Or God may intervene and upend the tables of nature's laws. Whatever it may be, it is hard to retain our images of what a heaven, and an everlasting life, might be like. In what sense can it be personal?

Yet personal, if we believe this last gospel in the Good Book, is what God, creation, and we ourselves are, in essence.

The beloved disciple gained confidence that he would, one way or another, stay with the Lord. The others were, with good reason, shaky. By the time of the beloved disciple's community, there was greater expectation. What remained for them, in the faith perspective of the beloved, was the likelihood of long life and the persistence of holy companionship. The indication that more would come and some would stay defined their church as well as their anticipated trajectory into the future. With so much more belief to grow and so much greater love ahead, the disciple, the writer, could only heave a long, closing sigh about what was left unsaid.

There would not be books enough, John wrote. There could never be time enough to relate the stories of Messiah and how they came to know him. The reader of John comes to expect that there was still, on the last day of his writing, and is still today, more to be written, more to be done, and more loving to be enacted, person-to-person. Jesus, the beloved's Love, lived and lives on. So there must be more of his loving to be known and shown. That would seem to require a lot of undying—for ourselves, for our sense of place, and for something of what we love as cosmos. How it might happen, though, who can predict? Who but the Timeless One can write the future story?

Jesus, Lord of the universe and the beloved's Love, whatever becomes of us and our world is your gift, your gracious will. Give me faith in the everlastingness of your promise that we ourselves and all that has been outpoured by your love will somehow live on. Be life in us. Be personal love. Be cosmic strength. Be life persistent.

For Reflection

Do I ever fear scientific scenarios of expansion into unimaginable (and unlivable) extremes or compression into super-dense lifelessness? Do I expect God to follow cosmic laws as we now think we know them? Do I allow for new discovery and for Spirit-breathed surprise?

Will I ever know, much less tell, enough of God's story? From my sense of God's action in creation, what do I expect to meet at the end of time? What themes and persons have I come to expect to be endless?

A Note Before the Epistles

Livvie, in Dorothea Benton Frank's novel *Sullivan's Island,* is matriarch and mammy. She's Sophia and queen of cornbread and hamhocks with turnip greens. She knows when to shush children and tell them just to listen up. She knows when to pooh away the hurts and insults of the day as stuff and nonsense. The adult woman who remembers her can second-guess how she'd judge this or that. Livvie would time just right the admonition that children needed to get hold of themselves. Yet she would also know when to open her arms, offer an ample head rest, and tell them, sugar, that troubles do weigh but they lighten when a helper can also carry them.

The church sometimes is and ought to be Livvie. The Johannine community found her, at heart, that way. Love was what church was all about—and Spirit, who, of course, was love. That was the simple key to survival. If someone needs, the church should lift a finger. If someone is persecuted, the church should buck them up. If someone doubts, the church needs to encourage. If someone is lost, the church ought to be way home. If someone has been misled, the church just needs to tell the truth. And if someone wants to hear about the Messiah, the church still needs to say, "We've seen him, we've touched him. Don't let anyone but him or anything at all carry you away."

That was what the three epistles were about. Two of them mention "an elect lady" who made way for all her children. Today they serve as call to be that again. To be church in the mode of that warm sand and okra soup and sweetgrass person.

The Witnesses

I John 1:1–4

We declare to you what we have seen and heard.

Mythmakers have set forth in search of Atlantis and El Dorado. Fortune hunters have panned gold in California rivers and mined silver in Nevada hills. Spiritual seekers have gone on pilgrimages to Fatima, Lourdes, Assisi, Rome, and the Holy Land. Knights who had won love tokens from fair maidens have gone on great quests for a sacramental symbol to seal their life and love, the Holy Grail. The beloved disciple and those who became his community needed none of this. He kept reminding them. Eyewitnesses to the ultimate were still alive. Dust kicked by Jesus' sandals still whisked around houses in the Galilean villages and on the road to Jerusalem. There was no need to wander, seek, treasure-hunt, or quest. The air they breathed bore God's breath.

Nothing could overshadow the power of personal experience, close and tangible. All that he knew of God's Son, all the awe he could muster, was summed up in his narrative. "We saw him, heard him, touched him. We were able to watch. He was one of us, had a beating heart, poured with sweat under the hot sun, enjoyed sitting with us at night near a fire when desert cold set in at the time of sunken light. There was nothing for us to do, no longer any unattainable goal, no more distracted pursuits before us because we somehow knew we'd met eternity in person."

Jesus' gaze had been loving, the community recalled to one

another. His words had been smooth and sure. His grasp had been sturdy. His whole body had spoken welcome home. All that could be left, the disciple forever wanted to say, was to invite more into their circle so that they, too, could know him.

There would always be room, he was sure, to bask in the here and now closeness of God-come-down. Jesus drew into holy family anyone who could imagine that God might breathe, sigh, smile, clasp a hand, and need company at night.

Sixty and seventy years later, that was still the wonder of it all. The wonder, the disciple surmised, could continue.

Multiply that by 33, 34, 35, and the wonder could get you 2100 more years. Multiply it again. Then imagine this word: *Infinity*. Or these: *Alpha*. *Omega*. The beginning and the end. Which is to say no end ever again. There was still, and that was the greatest miracle, a way to touch him.

Jesus, God-with-us, you are brother and son, fulfillment of us all and simple flesh and blood. Set my heart pulsing with your beat. Let me recount that I, too, have seen and heard and touched your love.

For Reflection

Dare I tell where and when?

Sin's Lightning

I John 1:5—2:17

If we walk in the light...we have fellowship with one another, and the blood of Jesus his Son cleanses us from all sin.

An episode of fainting, sinking into semi-consciousness with a severely low blood sugar, or blacking out after a blow to the head can make the dark of night a fearsome thing. We can feel ourselves pressed in a vise, barely able to breathe, as pitch black sets in. All we want is a gleam from somewhere to outline a doorway, reveal a faint form, restore our confidence that somehow we can find our way.

Sin, depression, grief, trauma, accident, injury, catastrophic illness, divorce, or the loss of love can enslave or paralyze us. We can feel trapped in a situation or in our own bodies. The experience of believing we have been loved and respected and then discovering that what we were promised was transitory or conditional can cast us into shadow and break our spirits.

Jesus, by word, by deed, by being, promised that no darkness, no shadow need ever envelop us finally. All sin is forgivable, all hurt is capable of healing, all that has been bent and broken is able to be rebuilt, all traps are able to be sprung. John was confident of this. God could only be light. This he had seen in Jesus.

God's love, mercy, immense understanding, unfaltering forgiveness would bathe us in light, he knew. Our lives could be sunshine and splendor. Our pain could be warmed into radiance. This also he knew.

Strangely, mysteriously, though, it required a bloodbath. The Lover-Son came to be wine, shine, and decree of freedom in his life sacrifice. How all that might work, the beloved disciple could not say with absolute clarity. That it was indisputably true, however, he would claim with all his might. The most fettered could and can go free. The most blind-folded could and can be unwrapped and could and can see.

Lord, forgive me my fear of the dark and free me from the pitch I've walked into. Set me alight with your love so I may again be confident and may tread lightly.

For Reflection

What fear persists in me? What darkness? How do I find Christ-light to lighten me?

Children and the Spirit's Abiding

I John 2:18—3:24

Little children, let no one deceive you.

There were liars and deceivers out there, antichrists galore. The newcomers to the faith, the baptized and newly anointed ones, had to be warned. It would happen. And though they were thoughtful adults, the writer of the epistle persisted in calling them children, little ones. In some sense, they were not far from being newborn.

The problem? Everywhere it went, the early church discovered that baptismal remission of sin didn't close the issue. Sin would reappear, in sheep's clothing, in messages about truth and knowledge and love. The neophytes and those far beyond would be hated by some, hounded by others. What the disciple reassured them of was the test of their hearts. "If our hearts do not condemn us," he said, "we have boldness before God" (3:21). He also pointed out to them that they needed not to have casual hearts or lax consciences. The best of what they had been called to and the best they knew of God, was to be obeyed if they were to be sure of their hearts.

Father Kenneth Himes has said this of sin in the Gospel of John: It is "a state of hostility between a stubborn, blind audience and Jesus." It is a counter-way, "a choosing of darkness over the light by refusing to believe in Jesus and enter into a relationship of discipleship" (Himes, "Human Failing: The Meanings and Metaphors of Sin," in *Moral Theology: New Directions and Fundamental Issues*, ed. James Keating). What is said of sin in the gospel is true of the epistles, too. It is not so much individual sins, the small offenses and unloving choices, as a deep-seated recalcitrance. Sin, at its heart, is a refusal to pledge personal allegiance to the Lord and is a deliberate deafness to the Word. Sin is hardness of heart against the birthing and rising of Love.

Soft hearts need not worry, though. They were the ones who were like children. They knew what they needed, knew what they didn't know, recognized their need for direction, were open to brothers and sisters, surrendered their selfishness, enrolled in the school of love.

Their world, like ours, was a world not only of children, humility, and innocence regained. It was a world, as is ours, where the falsely confident, the puffed-up, the heedless and heartless could still flash and glamorize and harm.

Unfortunately, what the community of the beloved disciple learned and kept having to learn again was that the Messiah had not converted everyone. He could not, because of his very nature, kill Cain.

Spirit of Jesus, come. Turn my voluntariness into a greater hearing and heeding. Give me a right and childlike heart to know you. Abide in me.

For Reflection

There is something in us, who tend to be sophisticates, that bristles at the put-down, the condescension, the intimation that we are thought inept, inadequate, or not quite grown up. We have been assured by our culture and its psychiatry that we need a healthy self-esteem. How can I have self-respect and confidence and still see myself as among "little children" in the realm of disicipleship?

God is Love

I John 4:1—5:21

"Everyone who loves is born of God and knows God."

It's all about community. It's fraternity and sorority in the root sense, not in the parlance of college and university. It's fellowship, family, bondedness at its best.

What the epistle-writer and his community had to face was that a Love-God would ask something of them. Their discipleship would not be just following rules, knowing holy words, giving religious gifts. It would be putting their lives on the line for the One who was Love incarnate and for all those he had given them—namely, one another.

Judith Lieu, a British scholar of the Johannine epistles, finds these recurrent and interrelated themes: mutual love; internal strengthening in grace and truth; banding together against apostasy and broken faith; doing righteousness in a world of opposition; being born from above; living in this world as though the next—and the fullness of God's kingdom—had already come.

The recipients of the letter were called by the God whose name and heart and being is Love. They were called, simply and clearly, to be heavenly people.

The miracle of it is that some, the leaders and healers and heralds among them, were sure that they could indeed be more than sign, more than semblance of God's reign. They could be "realized eschatology," living proof of the promised world, the life to come. Their "belief and behavior" could show forth Love by the coherence of their inner faith and outer works (Lieu, *The Theology of the Johannine Epistles*, pp. 109, 118).

They just needed these strong reminders about whose the world was, even though the enemy had taken it by storm and seemed, in dark moments, to have won. Love conquers. They needed to say it, and live it, in so very many ways, and again and again.

God, my whole life long I will never adequately know how to do love and how to be the love I live for. Teach me. Keep me. Help me know that it is in your community, your church, that we shun idols, reroute from our distractions, and bounce back from our deflections and defections from grace.

For Reflection

Why is it shocking to hear the stark declaration that God is love? What does it mean for me? What does it convict me of? What does it invite me to?

The Route of Love

2 John

And this is love, that we walk according to his commandments;
this is the commandment just as you have heard it
from the beginning—you must walk in it.

Along the south corridor of Interstate 81 in Virginia, there are ruins of barns, sheds, and mills along roiling creeks. Their warped and weathered boards are dented, bent, angled out where slats are missing. There are also, in the undulating valleys aside the Blue Ridge, grazing cattle, roll after roll of baled hay, autumn-bright trees, and a water tower, a few miles before New Market, freshly painted with the insignia of apples in a bushel basket. The farm route, rich in fences and siloes and wooded stretches just beyond farm ponds and chicken coops, also bears new human monuments—cellphone towers, the brick buildings and picnic pavilions of highway rest areas, and newly erected Comfort Inns, Sleep Inns, Hampton Inns, and Microtels.

One wonders whether the mix of old and new, natural and artificial is collision or coexistence. The community of the beloved disciple mused over similar phenomena. The old religion intersected the new, the chosen people intersected the empire. One could only wonder what might last and how.

When he wrote his letter to the "elect lady," such questions pressed not just upon John, or his spokesperson, but upon them all. Whether the lady was a woman leading a house church or was the code name for a whole community, the addressee was representative of those who were filled with wonderings. What had permanence? What and who, amidst rapid change, would survive? Wherein lay the secret of wherewithal and thriving? How spiritual could they be in a hyper-material world? How recalcitrant and irrelevant were they meant to be? And how did one go about loving resistance?

There was lasting truth, of that the disciples of the beloved disciple were sure. There was a path to truth, too, and that path was Jesus. He was God's Son and God's own, but he was also a human being who had walked in their midst. He had indeed risen, and so was not merely phantom or wish. He had taught and traveled and, in the end, proved triumphant. They awaited his return. When?

Meanwhile, they had to be reminded about progress, what it was and what it wasn't. "Anyone who is so 'progressive' that he or she does not remain rooted in the teaching of Christ," the epistle-writer chided, "does not possess God" (2 Jn:9, NAB translation). There was Christ and there were antichrists. There was progress and there was regress masking as advance.

The same could have been said to the members of the Way who gathered in Corinth or Thessalonica. And the message could have been repeated, a trifle later, in Carthage or Ethiopia. It could have been reiterated later still in Spain or South India or Sri Lanka. It could be splashed in news-rolling lights in Atlanta, at CNN headquarters, and in New York, at Herald Square, and along the East River, where the UN rises up in blue-green glass.

The message is still, that is to say, about the way we travel—God's way or otherwise. It is still about with whom we travel—true disciples or other smooth-talkers. It is still about who spells out the characters of our Mapquest—Jesus the Christ or some transient guru.

The writer would say the same of progress today, as we veer past Exit 245 and James Madison University, where a young man in a white jacket, wearing a black backpack, strolls across the bridge over the interstate, ambling wherever he's aimed early on a Monday.

God of the future and Lord of life to come, be progress in me and clear my eyes to see what's new of you.

For Reflection

Because Christianity is a religion of hope, sociologists and historians tend to say that the idea and ideal of human progress has been given life and energy by Christians. There is always a sense that this world can get better and be better, even as we prepare for life in the world to come. Christian nations, after all, have been scientifically progressive and technologically proficient. They have remodeled and reinvented themselves over and over. What progress am I sold on and devoted to? What progress ought I to question?

Another Little Letter

3 John

Beloved, I pray that all may go well with you and that you may be in good health, just as it is well with your soul.

You go to write or paint, to fish or weed, to survey a landscape or spot a sandpiper or indigo bunting. You go to have a heart-to-heart with a friend or to mutter to yourself about the follies of the universe. You go to watch a tide come in or to note how the garden grows colorful, plump, and green. You go to observe skywriting or to note how many are out strolling when they ought to be at work. You wonder whether their children ever go to school or how many of them know the stars that come and where, in that season's nights. You go to collect a wildflower bouquet, or a cache of shells, or your thoughts.

You go somewhere *not* to do. You go to let high tide or garden rain or insistent dusk steal over you.

There is much to be said about good doing and about doing good. We all do well to set goals, to measure results, to hold to high standards, to tally gains, and to write off losses, to record our learnings and remember what may be deadly to forget. It is good to work meaningfully and purposefully and to have a sense of mission. It is well for us to pursue truth. But it is also good to know when to rest and, believe it or not, know less. A time comes when the pen should be capped, the letter sealed, the e-mail closed, disposed, or reserved in a folder. It is high time, sometimes, just to wonder what might come next and to note that there are times it seems worthless to wish for anything.

The moment is, at times, enough. A child flops in surf. An old lady, surprisingly long in her skirts, drops down and rolls on her lawn, playing with the dog which is certainly as strong as she is. A church is set open so that souls can stop in one by one hoping for no music, no talk, no rustling of papers, no shuffling processions. At such times all one might want is candle flame.

Enough. Tide in, tide out. Sun down, sun up. Field in bloom, field gone a-stubble and the color of rust. Geese flying in their trenchant V, heron squatting in their startling high nests atop deadwood by a slow inlet or stream. Heart racing with passion, pulse needing the jump-start of pacemaker just to keep on. There is always the sun, yet only somewhat. Always, in our terms, is always less than the always of God.

There is something eternal about church. Not its principals or its present populations, not its problems or its praiseworthy projects. The eternal is its impulse, its faith. The beloved writer knew that there was beloved church—women, children, men who needed one by one a word of comfort, a hint of hope, a moment to stand still. Less than house or home, they needed the sanctuary of a still moment and a short note.

Which could leave them, for a little while, the welcome sense that there was nothing to be done.

But receive peace. But "greet the friends there" (verse 15). On a quiet day.

Give me sanctuary, good God, sufficient to keep sanity. Sufficient to restore my capacity to give and receive love. Let all go well with me, too—and soon.

For Reflection

When must I pause? Do I retreat regularly to regroup and refocus and recommit? Do I look for God and the good in all that I do, in all of my days?

What part does gratitude play in the life of love?

Closing Note

The Gospel and the Letters of John enroll a fascinating and incredible cast of characters. Some we come to know by name; some we would emulate; some we shake off sadly. Jesus spoke, and the beloved disciple spoke later of the past, the passing, and those to come.

Over all, from beginning to end, the Spirit wafts, enlivening, interpreting, loving up, posing future promise. It is the Holy Spirit, in the end, who empowers every believer and interprets for the church. It is the Spirit who brings us to our senses, such that we finally realize that there can never be words enough. It is the Spirit who tells us, as we learn Jesus syllable by syllable, deed by deed, presence by presence, that in the end one word is both synopsis and the whole story. That word, of course, is Love.

The whole of the gospel and the superscript of the three letters is one question: Do you?

Do I love? How? Whom? And why?

Will love, someday, when I grow up, be my enough?

For Further Reading

Brown, Raymond E. *The Community of the Beloved Disciple*. New York: Paulist Press, 1979.

Lieu, Judith M. *The Theology of the Johannine Epistles*. New York: Cambridge University Press, 1991.

Moore, Beth, with Dale McClesky. *The Beloved Disciple: Following John to the Heart of Jesus*. Nashville: Broadman and Holman Publishers, 2003.

Newheart, Michael Willett. *Word and Soul: A Psychological, Literary, and Cultural Reading of the Fourth Gospel*. Collegeville: Liturgical Press, 2001.

Smith, D. Moody. *The Theology of the Gospel of John*. New York: Cambridge University Press, 1995.

Vanier, Jean. *Drawn into the Mystery of Jesus through the Gospel of John*. New York: Paulist Press, 2004.